TORONTO

LORRAINE JOHNSON &
BARBARA HOPKINSON

EYEWITNESS TRAVEL

Left **View from the Toronto Islands** Right **Victorian houses, Cabbagetown**

LONDON, NEW YORK,
MELBOURNE, MUNICH AND DELHI
www.dk.com

Produced by
International Book Productions Inc., Toronto

Printed in China.

First published in the UK in 2005
by Dorling Kindersley Limited
80 Strand, London WC2R 0RL
A Penguin Random House Company

15 16 17 18 10 9 8 7 6 5 4 3 2

**Copyright 2005, 2015 ©
Dorling Kindersley Limited, London
Reprinted with revisions 2007, 2009,
2011, 2013, 2015**

A CIP catalogue record is available from the
British Library.

ISBN 978-1-40937-050-5

Within each Top 10 list in this book,
no hierarchy of quality or popularity is implied.
All 10 are, in the editor's opinion, of roughly
equal merit.

Floors are referred to throughout in accordance
with North American usage;
i.e., the "first floor" is at ground level.

MIX
Paper from
responsible sources
FSC™ C018179

Contents

Toronto's Top 10

The information in this DK Eyewitness Top 10 Travel Guide is checked regularly.
Every effort has been made to ensure that this book is as up-to-date as possible at the time of
going to press. Some details, however, such as telephone numbers, opening hours, prices,
gallery hanging arrangements and travel information are liable to change. The publishers
cannot accept responsibility for any consequences arising from the use of this book, nor for
any material on third party websites, and cannot guarantee that any website address in this
book will be a suitable source of travel information. We value the views and suggestions of
our readers very highly. Please write to: Publisher, DK Eyewitness Travel Guides, Dorling
Kindersley, 80 Strand, London, WC2R 0RL, UK or email: travelguides@dk.com.

COVER: Front – **DK Images:** Cylla Von Tiedemann bl; **SuperStock:** Robert Harding Picture Library/Roy Rainford
main; Spine: **SuperStock:** Robert Harding Picture Library/Roy Rainford b. Back: **DK Images:** Rough Guides/
Enrique Urange tc; **DK Images:** Francesca Yorke tl, tr.

Left **Ripley's Aquarium of Canada** Right **Lifeguard station, Ashbridges Bay**

Around Town

Streetsmart

Contents

Left **Galleria, BCE Place** Right **Princes' Gate, Canadian National Exhibition**

Key to abbreviations
Adm *admission charge payable*

TORONTO'S
TOP 10

TORONTO'S TOP 10

TOP 10 Toronto Highlights

Torontonians are justifiably proud of their vibrant and exciting metropolis. Canada's largest city and its financial hub, Toronto has a tremendous amount to offer, including a thriving theater, music, and arts scene, top museums, world-class restaurants and shops, a beautiful lakeside location with lovely beaches, and streets safe and inviting to walk in. Its cultural diversity – over 90 ethnic groups are represented in Toronto – enhances the urban experience.

Royal Ontario Museum 1
A treasure-trove of ancient mummies, exquisitely decorated period rooms, huge dinosaurs, stuffed birds, stunning Chinese art, and imposing Greek and Roman sculptures are among the many rewarding sights to be seen during a visit to this wonderful museum (see pp8–11).

CN Tower & Its Views 2
High-speed external elevators mounted on this, the tallest building in the Western Hemisphere, whisk you up 181 stories to an unforgettable view of the city (see pp12–13).

Toronto Islands 3
A short ferry ride from downtown, this chain of small islands provides a respite from summer heat with its beaches, picnic grounds, and amusement park (see pp14–15).

Art Gallery of Ontario 4
This fabulous museum is home to an excellent collection of Canadian art, including that of contemporary artist Michael Snow (below). There are also fine collections of Inuit art, French Impressionists, sculpture, photography, and prints (see pp16–17).

80 miles (129 km)

800 — yards – 0 – meters — 800

Casa Loma 5
Built by financier Sir Henry Pellatt, this turreted mansion, with its 98 grand rooms and beautiful gardens, provides a glimpse of turn-of-the-19th-century luxury (see pp18–19).

DUPONT

The Annex

BLOOR STREET WEST

AVENUE

COLLEGE STREET

SPADINA

Chinatown 4

KING STREET WEST

BATHURST STREET

SPADINA AVENUE

GARDINER EXPRESSWAY

GARDINER EXPRESSWAY

QUEENS QUAY WEST

LAKE SHORE BOULEVARD WEST

Dicover more at www.dk.com

Distillery Historic District
Once the largest distillery in North America, this former industrial complex is one of Toronto's hottest destinations. Victorian buildings and cobblestoned streets provide an unforgettable backdrop to the many unusual stores and galleries, and excellent restaurants and cafés found here (see pp20–21).

Ripley's Aquarium of Canada
Greet sharks, octopi, stingrays, and giant grouper in this impressive aquarium. A visit starts with the Canadian Waters gallery, home to an over 70-year-old lobster. (see pp22–3).

Toronto Eaton Centre
Toronto's pre-eminent downtown mall, named after a now-defunct department-store chain, is conveniently located near several major hotels and attractions. If you are looking for a one-stop shopping destination, this mall, selling everything from batteries to hockey sticks, is it (see pp24–5).

Hockey Hall of Fame
Irrespective of their age, most visitors to Toronto who are ice hockey fans make a pilgrimage here to see such revered relics as the original Stanley Cup, shoot pucks at a video goalie, walk through the re-creation of a locker room, and watch some of hockey's sterling moments in the Broadcast Zone (see pp26–7).

Niagara Falls
After the two-hour drive from Toronto, stand on Table Rock for a look at one of the world's wonders, the magnificent Horseshoe Falls, where the Niagara River plunges 176 ft (53 m) over a 1060-ft- (323-m-) long precipice. The town of Niagara Falls and outlying area offer fine dining, entertainment, winery tours, historic museums, and more (see pp28–31).

Yorkville
Queen's Park
Downtown
Toronto Inner Harbour
1 mile (1.6 km)

TOP 10 Royal Ontario Museum

Canada's largest museum, with more than six million objects, the Royal Ontario Museum, or ROM, was created in 1914 with the ambitious dual mandate of showcasing human civilization and the natural world. Galleries of archeology, science, art, world cultures, and natural history display significant collections of Chinese treasures, ornate mummy cases, and dinosaur skeletons. Hands-on exhibits invite children to excavate for fossils and examine species under a microscope.

Museum facade

🔵 Grab a quick bite in the cafeteria on Basement Level 1.

🟢 Visit 4:30–8:30pm on Fridays for discounted admission. The website details special programming, much of which is free.

• 100 Queen's Park; however, the main entrance is around the corner on Bloor St W. The museum is very close to both St. George and Museum subway stations
• Map C3
• 416 586 8000
• www.rom.on.ca
• Open 10am–5:30pm daily (until 6:30pm Fri)
• Adm: $16 adults; $14.50 senior citizens and students; $13 children aged 4–14; special exhibitions have a separate admission fee

Top 10 Features

1. Djedmaatesankh Mummy
2. *Barosaurus* Dinosaurs
3. Acropolis Model
4. Living Beehive
5. Mosaic Dome
6. English Parlor
7. Ming Tomb
8. Totem Poles
9. Chinese Guardian Lions
10. Hardwood Forest

1 Djedmaatesankh Mummy

Richly decorated with gold leaf and hieroglyphic inscriptions, this ancient Egyptian sarcophagus (below), which dates back to around 850 BC, protects the mummified body of a court musician. Although museum researchers have never opened the case, a high-tech CAT scan has revealed that she died at age 35 from a severe tooth abscess.

2 *Barosaurus* Dinosaurs

"Gordo", towering above the other specimens in the Temerty Gallery (above), is the largest dinosaur on display in Canada and, uniquely in the world, consists almost entirely of real fossils.

3 Acropolis Model

The Golden Age of Athens – about 400 BC – comes alive in this model of Greek temple life, which depicts the Parthenon and surrounding buildings as they looked at the height of ancient Greek civilization.

4 Living Beehive

This active beehive is a highlight of the Hands-On Biodiversity Gallery. Visitors can see the interior of the hive, buzzing with thousands of honey bees that have flown in from the outdoors.

Mosaic Dome
A spectacular mosaic dome tops the rotunda. Over a million tiny colored squares of Venetian glass form symbols of ancient cultures, such as an Inca thunder god and a mythical Greek seahorse.

Bloor St. main Entrance

Totem Poles
Four striking totem poles, the stylized figures commemorating family origins and achievements, were carved out of western red cedar in the 1880s by the Nisga'a and Haida peoples of Canada's northwest coast. The tallest is over 80 ft (24 m) high.

Chinese Guardian Lions
Two proud stone lions, carved for a Beijing palace in the 1600s, stand guard outside the museum.

English Parlor
Dating from the 1750s, with original carved pine walls and period furniture, this parlor *(right)* looks as if a wealthy English gentleman and his card-playing friends have only momentarily left the room. Though the gilded harp in the corner is silent, evocative, ambient Baroque music completes the vignette.

Ming Tomb
Guarded by stone camels, a fierce warrior, and a scepter-bearing adviser, this ensemble of funerary sculpture features artifacts from the Yuan dynasty (14th century), Ming dynasty (15th–17th centuries), and Qing dynasty (17th–18th centuries). Sculpted mythological animals adorn the arches.

Hardwood Forest
The dappled light and hushed calm of an Ontario hardwood forest are perfectly re-created in this diorama *(below)*. If you look closely, you will see more than 20 animals, among them a porcupine and fox, hiding among the colorful autumn leaves.

Key to Floorplan

■	Level 1
■	Level 2
■	Level 3

Museum Guide

Walkways on each level join exhibitions in the Crystal to the main building. Level 1 includes the Korea, China, and Japan collections, and galleries exploring the development of Canada as a nation – First Peoples and Canadian Heritage. Natural history is the focus of Level 2, with galleries on minerals and gems, evolution, and dinosaurs. Level 3 features anthropology and archeology, with artifacts from Africa, the Americas, Asia Pacific, Egypt, and Rome, as well as 20th-century art and design. Textiles and the Institute for Contemporary Culture are on Level 4. Temporary exhibitions are held in the Garfield Weston Exhibition Hall.

Left **Inuit coat, First Peoples Gallery** Right **Ming Dynasty headrest, Chinese Art Collection**

TOP 10 Collections

1 Dinosaurs
The popular Dinosaur Gallery, located on Level 2 in the Michael Lee-Chin Crystal, is home to almost 25 full dinosaur skeletons, of both marine and land dwellers, including the world's most complete *Maiasaura* and her baby, which are thought to be 80 million years old.

2 Hands-On Biodiversity
Children and adults alike are encouraged to get up close and personal with the wonders of the natural world in this imaginative discovery zone on Level 2. Touch animal skulls, antlers, and pelts, and don special glasses to look at the world through the "eyes" of various animals.

3 Canada's First Peoples
The ROM's holdings of Aboriginal artifacts, on Street Level, are superb. National treasures include an Innu-painted caribou-skin coat and a quilled pouch collected by Canadian painter Paul Kane (1810–71), who traveled among Native settlements in the mid-1800s. Don't miss the Umyak boat, large enough to hold an entire village.

4 Ancient Egypt
More than 1,000 artifacts, from everyday gold earrings to elaborate ceremonial mummy cases, combine to shed light on ancient Egypt (Third Level). The Punt Wall, a plaster cast taken from the temple of Queen Hatsheput near present-day Somalia, provides an opportunity to test your skill at decoding hieroglyphics.

5 Ice-Age Mammals
The rise of mammals following the Ice Age's "big chill," which ended about 10,000 years ago, is explored in this dramatic exhibit on Level 3. A giant beaver, mastodon, saber-toothed cat, and hippopotamus are just some of the impressive specimens on display.

6 Gallery of Birds
Hundreds of birds from all over the world swoop together in one spectacular flock, suspended in midflight from the ceiling on Level 2. Marvel at the 9-ft (2.7-m) wing span of the albatross *(left)*; listen to birdsongs at interactive booths; and pull out drawers containing nests, bones, eggs, and feathers.

7 Art Deco
Rare French and American Art Deco furniture, lamps, and sculpture – exquisitely crafted from ebony, lacquer, and ivory, among other fine materials – celebrate this influential design movement of the 1920s and 1930s. Art Deco glass, ceramic, and silver pieces round out this collection, on Level 3.

Discover more at www.dk.com

Top 10 Architectural Highlights

1. Rotunda
2. Totem Poles
3. Queen's Park façade
4. Stained-glass windows, Queen's Park entrance
5. Spirit House
6. Liza's Garden
7. Floor mosaic at entrance to Samuel European Galleries
8. Leaded windows in stairwells
9. Arched windows along western façade
10. Exterior cornice around building

The Crystal

The highlight of the museum's renovation is the Michael Lee-Chin Crystal, a magnificent addition designed by world-renowned architect Daniel Libeskind and named for the lead donor. This jagged crystalline structure of interlocking forms, with its spectacular atrium space, glass-sliver windows, and jutting angles thrusting over the sidewalk, now forms the dramatic entrance to the museum. Inside the Crystal, which has been designed to have no right angles, are four levels of galleries, including two unusual spaces: the Spirit House, a soaring void crisscrossed by bridges linking the newest galleries, and the Stair of Wonders, an intriguing vertical cabinet of curiosities from the ROM's collection. The Crystal is linked on all levels except the fourth to the original building.

The Michael Lee-Chin Crystal, with the historic building to the left

Chinese Art

8 Spanning over 6,000 years of Chinese history (4500 BC to AD 1900), this collection (Level 1) ranks among the world's finest. The procession of 7th-century ceramic tomb figures and the monumental Buddhist sculptures from the 12th to 16th centuries are outstanding.

Arms and Armor

9 On Level 3, intimidating battle gear stands guard over some 300 pieces – from 15th-century European chain mail to World War I automatic weapons – that high-light the history of human conflict.

Greek Sculpture

10 Striking stone, bronze, and ivory sculptures make this collection on Third Level one of the best in North America. Those dating back to the Hellenistic Age, around 325 BC, reflect the development of Greek society under Alexander the Great as his army forged into Egypt and India.

TOP 10 CN Tower & Its Views

A 58-second elevator ride whisks you to the 114th story of the tallest building in the Western Hemisphere, the 181-story, 1,815.5-ft (553.5-m) communications tower built by Canadian National Railway in 1976. Breathtaking views from the glass-fronted elevator set the stage for more dizzying sights from the LookOut, where on a clear day you can see as far as the Canada-US border. Visitors with nerves of steel can walk on the Glass Floor for a view 1,122 ft (342 m) straight down. For panoramic views 1,465 ft (447 m) above the ground, take an elevator up 33 more stories to the SkyPod, the highest observation level at the CN Tower.

The Glass Floor

🍴 Stop in at Horizons Café on the LookOut level for casual fare and spectacular views. Or reserve a table at the revolving 360 Restaurant (416 362 5411) to enjoy fine dining and a view that changes slowly throughout the meal.

🛍 Shop for one-of-a-kind souvenirs and authentic Canadiana at the Marketplace.

Test your nerve on the world's highest external walk on a building. CN Tower's EdgeWalk is a full-circle, hands-free walk on a 5-ft- (1.5-m-) wide ledge.

• 301 Front St W
• Map J5
• 416 868 6937
• www.cntower.ca
• Open 9am–10:30pm daily; closed Dec 25
• Adm: $32 adults; $24 senior citizens and children aged 4–12; add $12 for access to the SkyPod

Top 10 Views

1. Toronto Islands
2. Toronto Eaton Centre
3. Toronto Music Garden
4. Financial District
5. Urban Forest
6. Roy Thomson Hall
7. Union Station
8. City Hall
9. Fort York
10. Niagara Falls

1 Toronto Islands

A ribbon of islands *(above) (see pp14–15)* shelters Toronto's harbor and provides a car-free retreat just a short ferry ride from downtown. The islands have bike paths, picnic areas, beaches and boardwalk, and an amusement park *(see p49)*.

2 Toronto Eaton Centre

Tourists and locals alike flock here for the hundreds of shops and eateries *(see pp24–5)*. The glass vaulted roof is modeled on a 19th-century Italian galleria.

3 Toronto Music Garden

The garden's design, inspired by the music of Baroque composer J. S. Bach, is best seen from above; the swirling pathways and plantings do indeed seem musical *(below)*.

At the heart of City Hall's plaza is the Peace Garden. The roof of the structure within is "damaged," to symbolize world conflict

Financial District

Soaring towers, such as those of the modernist Toronto-Dominion Centre *(see p64)*, signal the heart of Toronto's – and Canada's – financial district *(right)*. The nation's major banks, insurance companies, and stockbrokers ply their trades as wind-jostled workers hurry along canyon-like streets.

Urban Forest

One look at Toronto from above and it's clear it's a green city: stately canopy trees line streets and snake along ravines.

Roy Thomson Hall

The space-age design of this music hall, in the core of the theater district, features a distinctive glass canopy *(see p44)*.

Union Station

A relic from the days when passenger rail was Canada's primary mode of transportation, this station *(above)* has lost none of its grandeur since it opened in 1927, still serving as an impressive gateway to the city.

Fort York

Founded in 1793 and the site of the 1813 Battle of York, in which the fort was destroyed and then rebuilt, Fort York *(right)* has Canada's best collection of buildings from the War of 1812 era. Eight original structures stand on this triangular piece of land, among them blockhouses, barracks, and officers' quarters. Many of the other buildings were torn down in the 1950s *(see p64)*.

City Hall

When opened in 1965, the building, with its two curving towers, was controversial in conservative Toronto; it has since become a much-loved icon of the city's modern architecture *(see p36)*.

Building Feats

One of the seven wonders of the modern world, the CN Tower is recognized as an unparalleled feat of 20th-century engineering. It took 40 months, with 1,537 workers toiling around the clock, to build the tower, pouring enough concrete to lay a sidewalk from Toronto to Kingston, 160 miles (260 km) away. A 10-ton Russian Sikorsky helicopter was used to lift the 44 pieces of the 335-ft (102-m) antenna into place.

Niagara Falls

If the weather cooperates, it's possible to see the mists rising above Niagara Falls, 80 miles (130 km) to the southeast *(see pp28–9)*. The gentle curve of land along the shores of Lake Ontario reveals why the region, which extends from Toronto to Niagara, is known as the Golden Horseshoe.

Toronto Islands

Originally a peninsula, the islands were formed when the rushing waters of the Don River separated a spit from the mainland during a ferocious storm in 1858. There are more than a dozen islets and mid-sized islands in this urban archipelago, some of them connected by bridges, others accessible only by boat. A thriving residential community of creative characters calls Ward's and Algonquin islands home, while Centre Island is a popular destination for its amusement park. No cars are allowed on the islands, adding enormously to their tranquil charm. Along with exploration on foot, two great ways to get the most out of the island experience are to rent a boat or a bicycle and paddle your way through the extensive lagoon system or cycle to a secluded picnic spot. It is easy to forget that you are right beside one of the busiest ports in Canada.

Cottage, Ward's Island

- There are fast-food spots and snack bars on the island but keep in mind that these are well spread out and have seasonal hours.

- Ferries depart from the terminal at the foot of Bay Street. Centre Island ferries operate in summer and fall; Ward's Island and Hanlan's Point ferries, year-round.

  The ferry ride ($7 for adults, $3.50 for children round-trip) takes about 10 minutes. Bicycles are permitted on board, except on the Centre Island boat if it is very busy.

- Map B6–E6
- Ferry schedule: 416 397 2628; www. torontoislands.org
- Bicycle rentals: 416 203 0009; www.torontoislandbicyclerental.com

Top 10 Features
1. Ferry
2. Boardwalk
3. Ward's Island
4. Gibraltar Point Lighthouse
5. Centreville Amusement Park
6. Far Enough Farm
7. Algonquin Island
8. Hanlan's Point
9. The Rectory
10. Bicycling

Ferry
Enjoy one of the best views to be had of the Toronto skyline *(center)* aboard a ferry dating back to the 1950s – some in the fleet even to the 1930s – as it chugs across the lake to the Toronto Islands.

Boardwalk
The 1.5-mile (2.5-km) boardwalk runs from Ward's Island to Centre Island and is great for a lakeside stroll *(below)*.

Ward's Island
Over 700 people now live here in what began, in the 1880s, as a tiny tent settlement. Stroll along the pathways and marvel at the creative ways the cottages have been ornamented to reflect their owners' tastes. As on neighboring Algonquin Island, the gardens of Ward's Island are in delightful bloom in the warmer months.

For more information on Toronto Islands ferries See p108

Gibraltar Point Lighthouse
Toronto's oldest lighthouse (left) has served as a shipping beacon since the early 19th century. The historic limestone landmark is rumored to be haunted by the ghost of its first keeper, who disappeared without a trace in 1815.

Centreville Amusement Park
This small amusement park on Centre Island has more than 30 rides, including swan boats (above) and a colorful 1890s carousel (see p49).

Far Enough Farm
Kids will love feeding and petting the lambs, goats, cows, pigs, and other farm animals at this small petting zoo.

Algonquin Island
Island residents' creativity is most exuberantly expressed in their quirky, colorful gardens. The green thumb enthusiasts of Algonquin Island are often happy to share their tips with passersby.

The Rectory
This cozy restaurant also functions as Ward's Island informal social center. Main courses, soups, salads, and sandwiches are healthy and hearty, and the desserts are delicious.

Hanlan's Point
Two sandy beaches, popular with sunbathers, are the big draw here. In 1999, one of the beaches reclaimed the clothing-optional status, which it enjoyed when it first opened in 1894 (see p51).

Bicycling
The best way to tour the islands is on wheels along the pedestrian-bicycle trails stretching the 4-mile (6.5-km) archipelago. Rent a one-person or tandem bike or quadracycle (right).

Canada's Coney Island

The heyday of Hanlan Point began in the 1880s as city dwellers flocked to its vaudeville theater, dance hall, hotels, and amusement park. Two decades later, thousands of fans cheered on baseball great Babe Ruth as he hit his first professional home run, on September 5, 1914, at the Point's new stadium. By 1937, however, the declining resort had been torn down to make way for the Island Airport.

TOP 10 Art Gallery of Ontario

Founded in 1900 and now one of the most prominent art museums in North America, the wide-ranging Art Gallery of Ontario (AGO) has over 80,000 works. The outstanding pieces of Canadian art, in particular paintings by the Group of Seven, are a national treasure. Along with superb Henry Moore plasters, bronzes, and other works, the gallery exhibits significant masterpieces of European art, from paintings by Tintoretto and Frans Hals to Vincent van Gogh and Pablo Picasso. More recent acquisitions include an impressive collection of African and Australian Aboriginal art. A major renovation, designed by world-renowned architect Frank Gehry, was completed in 2008.

The Grange

🍴 The AGO offers a lower level café with a family-friendly light lunch menu and upmarket Frank, where artful dining is embraced by pairing menus with exhibitions.

🛍 Browse the Gallery Shop for specialty gifts, reproductions from the gallery's collection, books, and handcrafted jewelry.

Join one of the free tours for extra insight into the collections and exhibits. Call the information line at 416 979 6648 for details.

• 317 Dundas St W
• Map J3
• 416 979 6648
• www.ago.net
• Open 10am–5:30pm Tue–Sun (to 8:30pm Wed)
• Adm: $19.50 adults; $11 youths and students; $16 senior citizens; $49 family ticket; under 5s free

Top 10 Collections

1. The AGO Kids' Gallery
2. Henry Moore
3. Group of Seven
4. French Impressionists
5. Contemporary
6. Canadian Collection
7. Thomson Collection
8. Prints and Drawings
9. Photography
10. Inuit Art

1 The AGO Kids' Gallery

This kid-friendly gallery has themed exhibitions geared at young visitors. There's also an activity centre, costumes, and a photo booth where kids can draw and pose for portraits of themselves.

2 Henry Moore

The world's largest public collection of works by British artist Henry Moore (1898–1986) encompasses bronze sculptures, plaster and bronze maquettes, drawings, and prints. His monumental *Large Two Forms (right)* broods outdoors, with its surface now worn smooth by admirers' countless rubbings.

3 Group of Seven

Iconic scenes of the Canadian landscape epitomize this deeply influential group of painters who strove, in the 1920s, to create a national artistic identity. The collection features signature work by A. Y. Jackson, Lawren Harris, and Tom Thomson *(center)*, who died before the group officially banded together.

→ *General admission to the gallery is free every Wednesday, 6–8:30pm; Separate admission fee for special exhibitions*

Contemporary
Accessed by the stunning wooden spiral staircase, this collection covers American and European art since 1900 and Canadian art since 1985. Canadian artists represented here include Betty Goodwin, Joanne Tod, and Elizabeth Magor. Conceptual artists include Michael Snow *(below)*, and Jeff Wall.

French Impressionists
Claude Monet *(above)*, Camille Pissarro, and Pierre-Auguste Renoir are just some of the 19th-century artists whose masterpieces grace this estimable collection.

Canadian Collection
These galleries include First Nations and Inuit art, and such Canadian luminaries as William Kurelek, Alex Colville, and Emily Carr.

Thomson Collection
The largest philanthropic cultural gift in Canadian history, these 2,000 works add remarkable depth to the AGO's collection, with emphasis on Tom Thomson and the Group of Seven, 19th-century painters Cornelius Krieghoff and Paul Kane, and the work of 20th-century radical abstract expressionists Paul-Émile Borduas and Jean-Paul Riopelle.

Prints and Drawings
The works in this collection range from the 15th to 21st centuries and include important Italian, Dutch, German, French, and British pieces. *Adam and Eve* (1504) by German etcher Albrecht Dürer *(below)* is a highlight. Works by Canadian artists also feature strongly. The Marvin Gelber Prints and Drawing Study Centre displays selected pieces.

Photography
This broad collection contains much early work, with a large contribution from Czech photographer Josef Sudek, plus albums from WWI and photographs taken in the 1930s and 1940s by the Klinsky Press Agency.

Inuit Art
This fine collection of works produced after World War II includes sculptures, prints, and wall hangings crafted from indigenous materials.

The Grange

At the south end of the gallery, the Grange was the first home of the AGO and was awarded National Historic Site status in 1970. The elegant Georgian mansion, the city's oldest standing brick house, was built in 1817, when Toronto was just the small town of York in Upper Canada. The house reflects the conservative British tastes of Upper Canada at the time with its symmetrical 5-bay facade and central pediment. The owners, D'Arcy Boulton Jr., and his wife, Sarah Anne, were prominent members of their community. An exhibition here recounts the story of the house and its former inhabitants.

Casa Loma

This Edwardian-style castle, completed in 1914 for a staggering $3.5 million, looms on a hill, overlooking downtown. Designed by famed Toronto architect E. J. Lennox (see p36), Casa Loma – Spanish for "house on the hill" – was the estate of prominent financier and industrialist Sir Henry Pellatt, who was forced by financial ruin to abandon his 98-room dream home less than 10 years after it was built.

Façade detail

🍴 Grab a bite at the Liberty Café, open daily.

🎧 Wander the castle on your own self-guided audio tour, available at no charge in eight languages.

The colorful estate gardens are open from May through to October, weather permitting.

• 1 Austin Terrace
• Map C2
• 416 923 1171
• www.casaloma.org
• Open daily 9:30am–5pm (last admittance 4pm); closed Jan 1 & Dec 25
• Adm: $24 adults; $18 senior citizens and youths (14–17); $14 children aged 4–13

Top 10 Features

1. Tunnel
2. Great Hall
3. Oak Room
4. Sir Henry's Study
5. Sir Henry's Bathroom
6. Conservatory
7. Towers
8. Gardens
9. Library
10. Round Room

2 Great Hall

The grand entrance hall *(below)*, with its 60-ft- (18-m-) high ceiling, sets the castle's tone of splendor. Gargoyles grin down on visitors from the pillars. Audio guide tapes are available here.

3 Oak Room

It took artisans three years to carve the magnificent French oak paneling in this stately drawing room. The ceiling's lavish plaster moldings conceal indirect lighting – the first time this type of lighting was used in a Canadian home.

1 Tunnel

Hidden 18 ft (5.5 m) below ground, an 800-ft (240-m) tunnel connects the castle to the carriage house and stables, where Sir Pellatt's horses were kept in grand style. An exhibit here, Toronto's Dark Side, tells the story of the city's darker days including the Prohibition, The Depression, and The Plague.

4 Sir Henry's Study

Look closely at the wood panels by the fireplace – they conceal two secret passages. The one to the right gave Sir Henry quick passage to the wine cellar, and his huge wine collection. Climb the one to the left and you'll reach the second floor, near his bedroom suite.

5 Sir Henry's Bathroom

Heavy on hedonistic comfort, the shower was designed to completely surround the body with sprays of water from above and from the sides, with six large taps controlling three levels of pipes. The walls are made of Carrara marble imported from Italy.

6 Conservatory

Magnificent bronze and glass doors, each set costing $10,000, are reproductions of a set made for an Italian villa. The intricate stained-glass ceiling dome, from Italy, was originally backlit by 600 light bulbs so that it glowed at night *(left)*. Beneath the conservatory lies a swimming pool that was never completed.

7 Towers

Stunning views reward those not afraid of heights. The east tower *(above)* is based on Scottish castle design; climb to the top and survey the property from its highest perch. The west tower, of Norman design, offers a breathtaking view of the city.

8 Gardens

Lavish gardens *(left)*, punctuated by sculptures and fountains, grace the estate with blooms during the growing season. Eight themed areas range from formal rose beds to woodland with luscious spring wildflowers. Don't miss the restored Potting Shed, its photo display chronicling the original gardens.

9 Library

Stripes of light and dark wood in the herringbone oak floor create an optical illusion of different shadings from each end of the room *(below)*. The elaborate plaster ceiling decoration features portrait busts and the family's coats of arms.

10 Round Room

With doors and windows custom-bowed to align with the curved walls, this room *(above)* is furnished with period pieces. Sir Pellatt's suite of ornately carved Louis XV chairs and folding screen are upholstered in rare French tapestry.

First in Luxury

As founder of the Toronto Electric Light Company, Sir Henry Pellatt brought electric power to the city, so it is not surprising that his home featured innovations that enhanced comfort on a scale never before seen in a Canadian home. Then-modern conveniences include an electric lighting system controlled from a panel in Sir Henry's bedroom, a central vacuuming system, forced-air heating, and the city's first electric elevator in a private home.

Distillery Historic District

Walking the pedestrian-only cobblestone streets past the best preserved Victorian industrial architecture in North America, you'll feel as if you've stumbled into another century. The 44 buildings of this 13-acre (5-ha) site were, until the mid-1900s, part of Gooderham and Worts, once the world's largest distillery. The distillery evolved from a grist mill founded here in 1832 by Englishman James Wort and his brother-in-law William Gooderham. The 150-year-old district has been infused with new life and is a vibrant community of cafés, restaurants, galleries, art studios, performance venues, and specialty shops.

Gooderham & Worts sign

Many of the restaurants and cafés have large patios set amongst the historic buildings. With no traffic or exhaust fumes, the Distillery District is a perfect place to dine on a summer evening.

Join a guided tour ($19) or a Segway tour ($39 for half hour; $69 for one hour) to get the most out of your visit. Details at www. segwayofontario.com or call 416 642 0008.

The district hosts many festivals and events throughout the summer and a popular Christmas Market in early December.

• 55 Mill St
• Map E5
• Take the 504 King streetcar or the Parliament St bus 65 from Castle Frank to King and Parliament, then walk south along Parliament • www.the distillerydistrict.com

Top 10 Sights

1. Caffe Furbo
2. Corkin Gallery
3. Mill Street Brewery
4. Boiler House Complex
5. Young Centre for the Performing Arts
6. Case Goods Warehouse
7. Balzac's Coffee
8. Thompson Landry Gallery
9. Arta Gallery
10. Bergo Designs

Caffe Furbo
Stop for a coffee at this quaint café in the heart of the district, occupying a building once used for canning industrial-grade alcohol. It now offers both a delicious selection of food and art to enjoy with it.

Corkin Gallery
Fronted with enormous windows to let in natural light – designed to diminish the fire hazard of producing alcohol under gas lighting – this 1873 building *(above)* is the perfect setting for the several art and photography exhibitions within.

Mill Street Brewery
While many of the Distillery buildings still smell faintly of the grain and alcohol once stored within, this 1879 building *(above)* renews its scent of malt and hops daily, from the Mill Street Brewery. Traditional handcrafted beers include an organic lager and a robust coffee porter. While sipping samples at the bar, check out the display of vintage distilling equipment.

Boiler House Complex
In the 1860s, the boiler house heated the entire distillery. Other buildings in the complex housed a carpentry shop, a blacksmith, and a canteen. They have now been converted into two restaurants with patio seating in summer, and the Brick Street Bakery.

Top contemporary Canadian artwork is featured in the Corkin Gallery and the Thompson Landry Gallery

Plan of Distillery District

⑤ Young Centre for the Performing Arts
Housed in Tank House number 9 and number 10, where whiskey was stored while it aged, is the main performance space of Toronto's largest theatre company, Soulpepper *(above)*.

⑥ Case Goods Warehouse
The majority of arts organizations and artists in the Distillery complex have their offices, work-shops, and studios in this building where cartons of liquor were once stored *(above)*. Many artisans display their unique works, including embroidery, jewelry, and handwoven clothing, in the boutiques here.

⑦ Balzac's Coffee
The pumps in this redbrick building led from the underground water reservoir, in case of fire; others were used for alcohol flow. It's now home to Balzac's Coffee *(below)*. Beans are roasted Mondays and Fridays.

⑧ Thompson Landry Gallery
This gallery, showcasing Quebec artists, is in a huge limestone structure, the complex's oldest. Its exterior retains features, such as a winch, from the days when the shore-line – and ships – came right up to the building.

⑨ Arta Gallery
Just off Parliament Street, and with the same old-world charm as the district itself, this gal-lery occupies a building that once housed a huge tank of molasses for rum.

⑩ Bergo Designs
Though expensive, this design shop has some of the most inter-esting items in the district: worth a browse.

Filming at the Distillery

When the Gooderham and Worts Distillery ceased operations in 1990, the entire site, with its evocative atmosphere, began a new life as the largest film set outside Holly-wood. With hundreds of film shoots here dur-ing the 1990s, including *Chicago*, *X-Men*, and *The Hurricane*, along with television series such as *La Femme Nikita* and *Alfred Hitch-cock Presents*, this was Canada's busiest filming location.

Ripley's Aquarium of Canada

Crouched at the base of the CN Tower, the hulking wave-like structure, Ripley's Aquarium opened in 2013. Inside, over 16,000 marine animals swoop, glide, and float within fresh and salt water tanks, all stunningly displayed, some several stories deep, others floating overhead. The aquarium is popular with children and the Discovery Centre here has plenty of play equipment for when the kids start to feel fished-out. Whether you're surrounded on all sides by saw-tooth fish or getting to know a zebra shark from a perspex bubble, you'll find the perspective at Toronto's first aquarium extraordinary and great fun.

Stingray

🍴 Light bites such as hot dogs, pizza, and coffee are available at Ripley's® Café.

🕐 During the school year, weekdays can be busier than you might expect. Avoid most school groups by arriving after 2pm.

• 288 Bremner Blvd
• Map J5
• 647 351 3474
• www.ripleyaquariums. com/canada
• 9am–11pm daily (some days closes earlier in the evening due to private functions; check website)
• Adm: $29.98 adults; $19.98 senior citizens and youths (6–13); $9.98 children aged 3–5

Top 10 Attractions

1. Fishes of the Great Lakes Basin
2. Pacific Kelp Viewing Tank
3. Rainbow Reef
4. Dangerous Lagoon
5. Discovery Centre
6. Sea Dragons
7. Perfect Predators
8. Piranhas
9. Stingray Bay
10. Pacific Sea Nettles

1 Fishes of the Great Lakes Basin

Bass, pike, carp, trout, and the comical long-nosed gar – local visitors especially may be surprised by how large the fish from the Great Lakes can grow *(below)*.

2 Pacific Kelp Viewing Tank

Waving strands of kelp rise up two storeys *(center)* providing a roomy home for over 25 species that swim off Canada's West Coast, including ling cod and rock fish.

3 Rainbow Reef

A sea of color awaits at this Indo-Pacific reef *(below)* where vibrant coral competes with neon species of fish.

Don't miss the aptly named Goliath Grouper in the Grouper Grotto, on your right about half-way along the Dangerous Lagoon tunnel

Dangerous Lagoon
A 315 ft (96 m) underwater tunnel takes visitors through the aquarium's largest tank *(above)* where sharks steal the show.

Pacific Sea Nettles
Stars of the Planet Jelly gallery *(below)*, these jellyfish put on a stunning display of contrasting colors in their backlit tank.

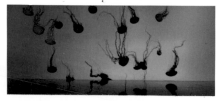

Plan of Ripley's Aquarium

Discovery Centre
Pet a horseshoe crab at the touch pool and surround yourself with clown fish in the peek-a-boo tanks *(right)*. A water table with locks, dams, and fish-runs demonstrates the complexity of shipping through the Great Lakes.

Sea Dragons
At first glance, you may only notice elaborate seaweed. Look again. Otherworldly weedy and leafy sea dragons float gracefully by *(below)*.

Stingray Bay
Southern, Cownose, and Roughtail rays appear to fly through the waters. The floor to ceiling tank gives the rays plenty of room to swoop and dive, skimming right past spectators' faces.

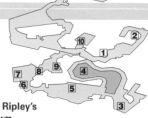

Key to Floorplan
■ Level 1
■ Level 2

Perfect Predators
Everything shark related is featured in this interactive gallery, from the power of a shark's bite to the contents of its stomach.

Piranhas
These deceptively peaceful, glittering predators have their very own tank.

Aquarium Guide
Displays start on the Upper Level with Canadian Waters. A curved ramp winds around the Pacific Kelp tank down to the Dangerous Lagoon. Visitors then find themselves in the Discovery Centre where there is a café. Galleries continue beyond the Discovery Centre past Perfect Predators and through Planet Jelly to the ramp heading back up to the Upper Level past the pumps and filtration systems of the Life Support System. Visitors exit via the Cargo Hold™ gift shop.

Toronto Eaton Centre

Named after Canadian retail legend Timothy Eaton – whose mail-order catalog and department store, Eaton's, was a beloved national institution until 1999, when the company declared bankruptcy. This multi-story shopping center is the quintessential downtown mall: big, busy, and boisterous. Opened in 1979 and heralded as the anchor that would transform down-at-heel Yonge and Dundas streets into an upscale destination, the complex houses some 230 stores, restaurants, and cafés.

Shoppers

🍴 The Urban Eatery in the basement at the north end of the mall has a range of food counters. Trinity Square Café, in the Church of the Holy Trinity, is open weekdays for lunch.

🛗 Ride the glass elevators, near the central fountain, for a great view of the galleria.

Navigate PATH using the color-coded signs: the red P steers you south, the orange A west, the blue T north, and the yellow H east.

• 220 Yonge St (with alternative entrances along Yonge St between Dundas and Queen, and at Queen St west of Yonge St)
• Map L3
• 416 598 8560
• www.torontoeaton centre.com
• Open 10am–9:30pm Mon–Fri, 9:30am–9:30pm Sat, 10am–7pm Sun; closed Easter Sunday and Dec 25

Top 10 Attractions

1. Flight Stop
2. Fountain
3. Galleria
4. Yonge-Dundas Square
5. The Labyrinth
6. Church of the Holy Trinity
7. Bronze Plaque
8. PATH
9. The Bay
10. Scadding House

Flight Stop
This sculpted gaggle of Canada geese by renowned Toronto artist Michael Snow – so life-like that you almost expect to hear the birds honk – is suspended from the vaulted ceiling of the central atrium.

Fountain
A focal point of the Toronto Eaton Centre, this waterburst fountain *(below)* lulls with soothing sounds of falling water and then astonishes as water shoots 100 ft (30 m) into the air. Encircled by benches, the fountain is a good spot to sit and take a break.

Galleria
Natural light pours through the soaring glass roof into the 865-ft- (265-m-) long arcade *(above)*. Designed by Eb Zeidler, the galleria is modeled on Milan's 19th-century Galleria Vittoria Emanuele. At the south end is The Bay department store while Nordstrom will locate here in autumn 2016.

Yonge-Dundas Square
Toronto's once-tawdry intersection is now a public square *(above)* embellished with 22 fountains set flush to the ground. Regular events take place on the square, especially during the summer months. The discount ticket booth TO Tix is located here.

Plan of Eaton Centre

The Labyrinth
This circuitous grass path is modeled on the 13th-century labyrinth at Chartres Cathedral in France.

Bronze Plaque
This historic plaque commemorates Yonge Street, ranked the longest street in the world by the Guinness Book of World Records. Yonge Street divides East and West Toronto and is the site of the city's first subway line.

Church of the Holy Trinity
This Anglican church dating to 1847 is as an oasis of calm amid commercial bustle. Admire the turreted entranceway while picnicking on the grounds; step inside to see the stained-glass windows.

PATH
From the Toronto Eaton Centre you can access the 27-mile (16-km) underground walkway PATH *(left)*. Linking several attractions, including the Air Canada Centre, Roy Thomson Hall, and Hockey Hall of Fame, PATH winds through stores and food courts.

The Bay
The Bay, founded by Hudson's Bay Company, is Canada's largest department store chain. It sells a wide selection of merchandise, such as home furnishings and fashion, but might be best known for its point blankets, first used in 1670 to barter for beaver pelts with the Cree. Its trading posts, based in the vast north of what is now Canada, were influential centers of commerce.

Scadding House
Built in 1857 for the Church of the Holy Trinity's first rector, this Georgian-Gothic house *(right)* was moved here to make way for the mall. The church and house, once surrounded by woodland, may be Yonge St's oldest building complex. The current rector lives in the house.

Hudson's Bay Company (HBC)

For 200 years, HBC controlled North America's lucrative fur trade. It was so powerful that it could make laws and wage war with Native tribes. After years of English-French battles over its posts, HBC lost its monopoly. In 1870, it sold its land to the Government of Canada. Turning to retail, HBC opened its first store in 1881, but kept a hand in the fur trade until 1991, when its last fur salon closed.

TOP 10 Hockey Hall of Fame

This shrine to Canada's favorite sport celebrates all things hockey, including those who have achieved greatness in the game. Housed in part in a beautiful former bank building dating to 1885, which is incorporated into Brookfield Place (see p36), the Hockey Hall of Fame contains the most comprehensive collection of hockey artifacts and memorabilia in the world, among them the original Stanley Cup trophy. Interactive exhibits run the gamut from multimedia trivia kiosks that test your hockey knowledge to a virtual reality puck-shooting game that allows visitors to go one-on-one against legendary players.

Hockey Hall of Fame façade

🍴 Many of the eateries in Brookfield Place *(see p36)* have seating in the spectacular galleria. A food court on the lower level provides quick snacks for those on the go.

⏱ If your energy flags, take a seat in either of the Hall of Fame's two theater venues to watch a retrospective highlights video or an interactive multimedia presentation.

• 30 Yonge St (enter through Brookfield Place concourse)
• Map L5
• 416 360 7765
• www.hhof.com
• Open daily (hours vary seasonally so call ahead); closed Jan 1, Dec 25 and induction day.
• Adm: $18 adults; $14 senior citizens; $12 children, under 3s free

Top 10 Highlights

1. Stanley Cup
2. Great Hall
3. Be a Player Zone
4. *Our Game*
5. Double Gold Olympic Exhibit
6. Broadcast Zone
7. Goalie Mask Exhibit
8. Montreal Canadiens Locker Room
9. Movie Theatres
10. Spirit of Hockey Shop

Stanley Cup
One of the world's best-known sports trophies, the original Stanley Cup *(above)* is on display here, as is the current one. Named for Canada's sixth Governor General, who proposed a yearly challenge cup, it was first presented in 1893.

Be a Player Zone
On a faux ice rink, with arena boards and multimedia scoreboard, shoot a puck at a life-sized video projection goalie, or be the goalie facing simulated shots by greats Wayne Gretzky and Mark Messier.

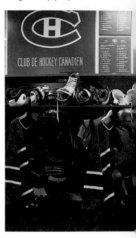

Great Hall
Players and icons of hockey are celebrated in this 45-ft- (14-m-) high former banking hall *(below)*. Giants of the game appear on the Honoured Members Wall, and all major NHL trophies are on display. You can have a photo taken with the Stanley Cup.

Not until its inclusion in the 1920 Olympics and the formation of the NHL in 1934 was hockey seen as serious sport rather than recreation

4 Our Game

Exuberant young players leap over the boards for a hockey game in this larger-than-life bronze sculpture by Ontario artist Edie Parker. Located just outside the museum at the corner of Yonge and Front streets, it is a popular backdrop for photographs.

Key to Floorplan

▪	Main Level
▪	Upper Level

5 Double Gold Olympic Exhibit

Featuring artifacts from both the Men's and Women's Vancouver 2010 Olympic hockey teams, including gold-medal winning puck.

6 Broadcast Zone

Use a high-tech navigational interface – just point and it plays – to custom-design your tour of great moments in hockey broadcast history, from early radio clips to present-day television excerpts. A highlight is the broadcast of the tension-filled last seconds of the 1972 World Summit Series, in which Canada scored on Russia.

7 Goalie Mask Exhibit

From a leather mask worn in the 1930s to one exemplifying today's sophisticated engineering, this display includes many strange examples of face protection *(right)* that have been personalized by goalies over the years.

8 Montreal Canadiens Locker Room

The only thing missing from this re-created locker room *(above)* from the old Montreal Forum is the players. Their jerseys and equipment are jumbled about, as if they might swoop in any moment to suit up.

9 Movie Theatres

Take a seat in either of the Hall of Fame's two theatres and catch highlights and full-length games from past to present. You can also sit back and enjoy hockey's first 3-D movie, Stanley's Game Seven.

10 Spirit of Hockey Shop

The museum's exit takes visitors through this shop. Hockey-themed merchandise includes a wide selection of team jerseys, sticks, and smaller items such as mugs and cups emblazoned with logos.

Canada's Game

Although several countries claim to have invented ice hockey, Canada calls the game its own. Even so, its origins are hotly contested. Students at King's College in Windsor, Nova Scotia, are said to have put puck to ice in the early 1800s. Others credit Micmac Indians in Nova Scotia, also in the early 1800s. Whatever the origin, British soldiers stationed at the Halifax, Nova Scotia, garrison were playing the game by the 1850s, as were military men in Kingston, Ontario.

Niagara Falls

One of the world's most famous natural attractions, the great arcs of hissing, frothing water crashing over cliffs 20 stories high is a dazzling spectacle. Drifting spray adds to the excitement of being near the edge of a stomach-churning drop. The 188-ft- (57-m-) high Canadian Horseshoe Falls is the mightiest of the three cataracts that make up Niagara Falls. Across the Niagara River is the impressive American Falls, including the smaller Bridal Veil Falls. When visiting the falls, be sure to make time to stop at some of the other sights in the Niagara region, including its renowned vineyards and historic museums.

Hornblower boats

🍴 For fine dining with views of the falls, head to Windows by Jamie Kennedy in the Sheraton on the Falls (5875 Falls Ave, 1866 374 4408).

🚌 The Adventure Pass covers admission to the *Hornblower*, Journey Behind the Falls, White Water Walk, and sensory experience Niagara's Fury. It also covers the WEGO bus which rides between many of the attractions.

• Map Q3
• www.niagarafalls tourism.com
• Tourist Office: 5400 Robinson St; 905 356 6061 or 1 800 563 2557
• Discount passes available – visit website for details; Voyage to the Falls: $19.95 adults; $12.25 children

Top 10 Attractions

1. Voyage to the Falls
2. Journey Behind the Falls
3. American Falls
4. Horseshoe Falls
5. Whirlpool Rapids
6. Table Rock
7. The Old Scow
8. White Water Walk
9. Butterfly Conservatory
10. Niagara Parks Botanical Gardens

Voyage to the Falls

Experience the falls from below aboard one of *Hornblower's* Niagara Cruises. The classic 30-minute voyage takes you to the Great Gorge, the American Falls, Bridal Veil Falls, and finally into the spray and rolling waters of Horseshoe Falls. You will be soaked, despite the courtesy rain poncho.

Journey Behind the Falls

Rock tunnels behind the Horseshoe Falls lead you past a wall of water so thick it blocks out daylight. The vantage point, well below the gorge's rim, is awe-inspiring *(right)*. Rain ponchos are provided – and necessary.

American Falls

New York State, on the US side of the international border, lays claim to this cataract, which has a total vertical drop 10 ft (3 m) greater than that of Horseshoe Falls. However, its 950-ft- (290-m-) wide crest and 2-ft (0.6-m) depth sees only a fraction of the volume of water that the Horseshoe Falls carries. It is easily seen from Table Rock.

Horseshoe Falls

This 2,200-ft- (671-m-) wide, 20-story cataract is formed as 90 percent of the water of the Niagara River, the natural outlet from Lake Erie to Lake Ontario, roars over a semi-circular cliff of the Niagara Escarpment *(above)*. Water tumbles some 10 ft (3 m) deep at the falls' center.

Brightly colored lights illuminate the falls during the spectacular Winter Festival of Lights (mid-Nov–mid-Jan)

Whirlpool Rapids

A sharp turn in the river just downstream of the falls creates a raging whirlpool, one of the most lethal stretches of water in North America. Daredevils can look down on the rapids from the Whirlpool Aero Car *(above)*, a 1913 cablecar traversing the shores.

Butterfly Conservatory

The butterfly conservatory is a huge heated dome with thousands of colorful creatures *(above)* flitting freely about – and sometimes landing on delighted visitors.

Niagara Parks Botanical Gardens

These beautiful gardens, located 6 miles (9 km) from the falls, include a splendid rose display that features more than 2,000 varieties.

Table Rock

Stand mere feet from the brink of Horseshoe Falls, a rail the only thing between you and a torrent of water. The lookout point was so named because its surface extended above the gorge like a table leaf. Deemed unstable in 1935, the ledge was blasted off.

The Old Scow

Stranded on rocks mid-river is this barge, shipwrecked in 1918. The two-man crew survived but had to wait 29 hours near the brink of the falls before being winched to safety. The best view is on an aerial tour *(see p31)*.

White Water Walk

Descend from the top of the chasm by elevator to a tunnel leading to a riverside boardwalk *(below)*. The whirlpools and rapids here are some of the most spectacular, and treacherous, in the world.

Forceful Flow

The forces of erosion that created the falls today wear them away. Before hydroelectric stations were built on the Niagara River, the rock face eroded by up to 6 ft (1.8 m) a year. Now it is just 1 ft (30 cm) annually. Almost a fifth of the Earth's freshwater flows over the falls – so much that it would take you an hour to fill a ditch running between Canada's east and west coasts.

In winter, an ice bridge spanning the riverbanks – up to 50 ft (15 m) deep – and small icebergs are an awesome sight

Left **Old Fort Erie** Right **MarineLand**

Fun Things to Do Around Niagara

1 Fort George
This historic British fort, built in 1796, was a key defense post during the War of 1812 between Britain and the US *(see p64)*. It has been restored to the period with replica buildings and costumed staff. ◈ *51 Queen's Parade, Niagara-on-the-Lake • Map Q3 • 9095 468 6614 • Open May–Aug: 10am–5pm daily; Sep–Apr: noon–4pm Sat & Sun • Adm*

2 Fallsview Casino Resort
Try your luck at the largest gaming resort in Canada, complete with 3,000 slot machines, 130 gaming tables, hotel, spa, shops, and restaurants. ◈ *6380 Fallsview Blvd, Niagara Falls • 1 888 325 5788 • Open 24 hrs daily*

3 Queenston Heights Park
A monument pays tribute to General Brock, a leader of the British forces killed in battle here during the War of 1812 *(see p64)*. With great views of Niagara River, the park is a fine picnic spot.
◈ *Niagara River Pkwy, Niagara Falls*

4 IMAX Theatre Niagara Falls
Don't miss the awe-inspiring *Niagara: Miracles, Myths and Magic,* chronicling the history of the falls. Projected onto a giant screen, the movie makes you feel like you're right in the midst of things. Original stunt barrels are displayed in the theater's Daredevil Gallery. ◈ *6170 Fallsview Blvd, Niagara Falls • 866 405 4629 • www.imaxniagara.com*

5 Skylon Tower
Its viewing deck affording vistas of as far as 80 miles (130 km), this tower rises 775 ft (236 m) above the falls. Fine dining at the revolving restaurant. ◈ *5200 Robinson St • 905 356 2651 • Open summer: 8am–midnight daily (from 9am in winter) • Adm*

Skylon Tower

6 Welland Canal
Linking Lakes Ontario and Erie, this eight-lock, 27-mile (43-km) canal opened in 1829, allowing vessels to traverse the Niagara Escarpment – and the 328-ft (100-m) height difference between the lakes. The canalside trail from Thorold to St. Catharines is great for ship-gazing. ◈ *Lock 3 Viewing Complex & Museum: Government Rd, St. Catharines • Map Q3 • 1 800 305 5134 • Open 9am–5pm daily*

7 Clifton Hill
This is the centre of Niagara Falls' entertainment: museums, mini-golf, and midway are just the start. Also, hotels and restaurants for every budget. ◈ *Niagara Falls*

Ship passing through Welland Canal

A fascinating full-day "Crossing Point Tour" covers Black history in the Niagara Region; visit www.niagaraboundtours.com

Top 10 Niagara Daredevils

1. Jean Francois Gravelot, aka The Great Blondin, tightrope crossing, 1859
2. Guillermo Antonio Farini, aka The Great Farini, stilt tightrope crossing, 1864
3. Henry Bellini, tightrope crossing and leap into river, 1873
4. Maria Spelterini, first woman to cross on a tightrope, 1876
5. Carlisle Graham, first man over the falls in a barrel, 1886
6. Clifford Calverly, fastest tightrope crossing, 1887
7. James Hardy, youngest tightrope crosser, 1896
8. Annie Edson Taylor, first woman over the falls in a barrel, 1901
9. Lincoln Beachy, first airplane stunt at falls, 1911
10. Nik Wallenda, tightrope crossing, 2012

The Great Blondin
Blondin's 1859 tightrope crossing of the Niagara River, his manager on his back.

Daredevil Feats

For some 200 years, daredevils have risked their lives at Niagara Falls for a chance at fame. Nineteen have died; many others have had close calls. The first daredevil, Sam Patch, dove headfirst from an 85-ft (26-m) high platform into the churning Niagara River, in 1829, and survived. Ten days later he did it again, from a height of 130 ft (40 m). The Great Blondin couldn't get enough of the falls, crossing the gorge on a tightrope nine times in 1859 – once carrying his manager. When Blondin returned in 1860 for more stunts, such as pushing a wheelbarrow across the rope, he was challenged by a young upstart, The Great Farini, who crossed carrying a washing machine. Farini performed biweekly, becoming increasingly daring – doing headstands, hanging by his toes. He survived them all and died at age 91. The first woman funambulist, Maria Spelterini, also crossed blindfolded, in 1876. The first woman to survive going over the falls in a barrel was Annie Taylor, in 1901. Emerging from her battered vessel, the 63-year-old schoolteacher said, "Nobody ought ever do that again," advice dozens have since ignored.

Niagara Helicopter Tour
8 Experience the exhilaration of swooping over the falls.
Niagara Helicopters (10 mins), 1 800 281 8034; National Helicopters (20 mins), 1 800 491 3117

Old Fort Erie
9 This reconstructed fort, a supply base for British troops in the 1700s, was the site of many battles with US forces in the 1800s.
350 Lakeshore Rd, Ft Erie • Map Q3 • 905 871 0540 • Open mid-May–Oct: 10am–5pm daily • Adm

MarineLand
10 Killer whales and Arctic belugas aren't the only attractions at this theme park. Walruses, dolphins and sea lions also make appearances in the marine animal shows; and there are bear, elk, and deer habitats. Adventurers can hop on the 10-plus rides, including the world's largest looping roller coaster and the only one with a bowtie inversion. 7657 Portage Rd, Niagara Falls • 905 356 9565 • Admission booths open 10am–5pm late May–mid-Oct, park open until nightfall • Adm

Niagara is known for its top vineyards **See p100**; most offer tours, tastings, and wines for sale; visit www.winecountryontario.ca

Left **Ontario Science Centre** Right **McMichael Canadian Art Collection**

🔟 Museums & Art Galleries

Art Gallery of Ontario
Reflecting some 600 years of human creative endeavor, the gallery's permanent collection contains more than 80,000 works in all media. The Canadian collection is particularly impressive *(see pp16–17)*.

Royal Ontario Museum
Canada's foremost museum offers an excellent balance of art, archeology, science, and nature, and has more than six million artifacts in its collections *(see pp8–11)*.

Robe, Textile Museum

Ontario Science Centre
The hundreds of interactive exhibits here make science fascinating and fun. Youthful visitors can touch a tornado, navigate their way in a rocket chair, explore the hair-raising effects of electricity, send paper whooshing up a wind tunnel, and construct ramps and loops for balls to whiz around on *(see p91)*.

Gardiner Museum of Ceramic Art
This museum was founded in 1984 by private Canadian collectors George and Helen Gardiner to showcase their extraordinary collection of pre-Columbian American pottery and European porcelain. Later additions have included Asian ceramics and contemporary artwork *(see p76)*.

Design Exchange
Located in the magnificent former Toronto Stock Exchange building, an Art Deco gem built in 1937, this center celebrates postwar Canadian design. Furniture, housewares, sportsgear, and medical equipment are among the items in the permanent collection and highlight the role of design in daily life. The center also hosts major national and international exhibitions. A gorgeous mural on the upstairs Trading Floor depicts Canadian industrial themes *(see p66)*.

Textile Museum of Canada
A permanent collection of over 10,000 fabrics, quilts, ceremonial cloths, and carpets from around the world are housed in this small but excellent museum. Temporary contemporary exhibits round out the historical artifacts. ⬥ 55 Centre Ave • Map K3 • 416 599 5321 • Open 11am–5pm daily; (until 8pm Wed) • Adm • www.textile museum.ca

McMichael Canadian Art Collection
The outstanding Group of Seven collection is the treasure of this gallery. The Group endeavored, in the early 20th century, to express a distinctive national identity through their paintings of the Canadian wilderness *(see p91)*.

Previous pages **Grand Parade, Caribbean Carnival**

Power Plant
Contemporary Art Gallery

Known for its boundary-pushing exhibitions of contemporary Canadian and international art, this edgy, non-collecting gallery features rotating shows of consistently high quality. If the art sometimes mystifies visitors, at least a building is instantly recognizable: a brick smokestack tops the 1920s converted power station *(see p66)*.

Toronto Dominion Gallery
of Inuit Art

As Inuit tool makers turned their skills to sculpting, the culture experienced a renaissance, this time in artistic achievement. Most of the 200 pieces in this gallery specializing in postwar Inuit sculpture are carved soap-stone, each evocative of the landscape, culture, and legends of the indigenous people of Canada's harsh Arctic region. The gallery's design echoes that of the TD Bank Tower, by renowned modernist architect Mies van der Rohe *(see p66)*.

Bata Shoe Museum

This unusual building, resem-bling a stylized shoebox, houses more than 13,000 artifacts, covering 4,500 years of footwear history. Artifacts represent an unparalleled range, from Ancient Egyptian funerary shoes (1500 BC) to 19th-century Nigerian camel-riding boots to Elvis Presley's patent blue loafers *(see p74)*.

Bata Shoe Museum

Top 10 Small Museums

1 Gibson House Museum
Elegant 1851 Georgian farm-house *(see p92)*.

2 Mackenzie House
Home of Toronto's first mayor (1834) *(see p83)*.

3 Toronto's First Post Office
A historic museum and work-ing post office *(see p84)*.

4 TIFF Bell Lightbox
Film-focused exhibitions at the HQ of the Toronto Inter-national Film Festival. ◈ 350 King St W • Map J4 • 416 599 8433 • Open Tue–Sun • Adm

5 MOCCA
Promotes innovative works by emerging artists. ◈ 952 Queen St W • Map B4 • 416 395 0067 • Open Tue–Sun • Free

6 Redpath Sugar Museum
Next door to a refinery, it tells the history of sugar production. ◈ 95 Queens Quay E • Map M6 • 416 933 8341 • Closed Sat, Sun

7 Campbell House
Oldest remaining building (1822) in the city *(see p75)*.

8 University of Toronto Art Centre
Impressive art collection behind University College. ◈ 15 King's College Circle • Map L2 • 416 978 1838 • Closed Mon & Sun • Free

9 Toronto Police Museum and Discovery Centre
Interactive displays, fascinating police artifacts, and exhibits chronicling infamous crimes. ◈ 40 College St • Map L2 • 416 808 7020 • Open Mon–Fri • Adm

10 CBC Museum
Celebrates the people and programs of Canada's national broadcaster. ◈ 250 Front St W • Map J5 • 416 205 5574 • Free

Left **Union Station** Right **Trinity College, University of Toronto**

⁝10 Architectural Highlights

1 Brookfield Place
Spanish architect Santiago Calatrava designed the striking atrium of this 1990 office complex. Its steel-and-glass canopy creates enchanting patterns of light and shadow. Façades of 19th-century buildings have been preserved in the Yonge Street frontage. ◈ 181 Bay St • Map L5

2 Toronto-Dominion Centre
Two austere, perfectly proportioned towers and a single-story pavilion of glass and black metal are Toronto's only design by International Style architect Ludwig Mies van der Rohe (1886–1969). Completed in 1971, the complex spurred the skyscraper boom that gave birth to the city's financial district. Four more towers were later added *(see p64)*.

3 CN Tower
Defining the skyline, Toronto's most recognizable architectural icon is also the tallest building in the Western Hemisphere *(see pp12–13)*.

4 University of Toronto
Founded in 1827 as King's College, this institute has many refined, stately buildings, such as the Romanesque Revival-style University College *(see p76)*.

5 City Hall
Causing a significant stir in 1960s Toronto, the design of New City Hall is bold, daring, and unique. Finnish architect Viljo Revell's two curving towers seem to embrace the central domed structure between them. A sweeping public plaza out front, Nathan Phillips Square, is the symbolic heart of the city *(see p75)*.

City Hall

6 Old City Hall
Now a courthouse, this Richardsonian Romanesque building, completed in 1899, was designed by the architect responsible for many of Toronto's grandest historic buildings, E. J. Lennox. For the best view of the clock tower, look north up Bay Street *(see p76)*.

Old City Hall

Dozens of architecturally significant buildings invite in the public every May during Doors Open Toronto; visit www.doorsopen.org

Sharpe Centre for Design

Top 10 Public Art Sites

1 The Pasture
Joe Fafard's seven bronze, life-size cows in gentle repose. ⊗ 77 King St W • Map L4

2 Three Way Piece No. 2
Aka *The Archer*, this Henry Moore bronze, controversial when installed in 1966, is now a local favorite. ⊗ Nathan Phillips Sq • Map K3

3 Wall and Chairs
Curved walls intersected by a triangle of three chairs echo the severe beauty of city towers. ⊗ TD Centre • Map K4

4 Toronto Sculpture Garden
Rotating exhibits of contemporary site-specific works. ⊗ 115 King St E • Map L4

5 Red Canoe
A huge canoe atop a mound with views over the Gardiner Expressway to Lake Ontario. ⊗ Canoe Landing Park • Map H5

6 Search Light, Star Light, Spot Light
Three hollow metal columns are pierced by hundreds of stars; lit from within, they glow like searchlights. ⊗ Air Canada Centre • Map K5

7 Untitled (Mountain)
A gorgeously layered aluminum sculpture, cut with water jets, by Anish Kapoor. ⊗ Simcoe Park • Map J4

8 The Audience
"Fans" spill out of the Rogers Centre in this frieze by Michael Snow. ⊗ Map J5

9 Woodpecker Column
Woodpeckers strike at a 100-ft (30-m) column. ⊗ 222 Bremner Blvd • Map J5

10 City People
Colorful aluminum figures spin softly in the breeze. ⊗ Royal Bank Plaza • Map K4

7 Sharpe Centre for Design
Propped up on 100-ft (30-m) stilts, British architect Will Alsop's addition to the Ontario College of Art and Design is playful and audacious. The two-story "tabletop" building connects to the main building via a sloping tunnel. ⊗ 100 McCaul St • Map J3

8 Royal Bank Plaza
The 14,000 mirrored windows of the two towers (1977) are insulated with 24-karat gold – $70 worth on each window, for a total of some $1 million, money saved on heating. ⊗ 200 Bay St • Map K4

9 The L Tower
Neighbouring the Sony Centre *(see p44)*, this 58-story skyscraper of condos was designed by Studio Daniel Libeskind. Its towering curve makes it the most elegant high-rise in the city. ⊗ 22 The Esplanade • Map L5

10 Union Station
The Great Hall of this 1920s monumental stone railroad station has an 88-ft- (27-m-) high vaulted ceiling. ⊗ 65 Front St W • Map K5

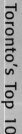

The Ontario Legislative Building is open to the public; watch politicians in action from the gallery or join a free tour (call 416 325 0061) 37

Left **Boardwalk, The Beach** Right **Cabbagetown**

Neighborhoods

The Beach
A charming enclave east of Woodbine Ave full of fun for the outdoor enthusiast, including those who consider shopping a sport. Browse the eclectic shops or relax in one of the many cozy restaurants or pubs *(see p93)*. Just south of the Queen Street East strip, a popular boardwalk stretches alongside a sandy beach to Ashbridges Bay *(see p40)*.

Chinatown
With one of the largest ethnic Chinese populations of any North American city, it's not surprising that Toronto has several Chinatowns, though none other as old as this one, settled in the early 1900s. Originally farther east on Dundas Street, the hub is now Spadina Avenue, where scores of shops and restaurants – including many Vietnamese ones – rub shoulders. The area is even more frenetic during Chinese New Year celebrations, usually in February *(see p73)*.

Chinatown signs

Cabbagetown
Settled in the 1840s by Irish immigrants who grew cabbages in their front gardens to help make ends meet, this area east of Sherbourne St between Wellesley St E

and Gerrard St E is today almost completely gentrified. Pretty cottages and Victorian rowhouses, along with upscale boutiques and gourmet shops, are well worth exploring *(see p83)*.

Little Italy
Most of the 500,000 Italians who call Toronto home now live north of the city, but the pizzerias, and *trattorias* that remain on this once predominantly Italian strip of College St west of Bathurst St ensure it retains its flair. At night, music and patrons spill out of trendy bars and restaurants *(see p76)*.

Yorkville
Famous in the 1960s as a hippie hangout and now the city's most exclusive retail district, this window-shoppers' paradise abounds with temptation. Refined art galleries nestle among chic boutiques, bars, and restaurants. Visiting movie stars can often be spotted here, especially during film festival time *(see p74)*.

Yorkville

The Danforth
6 This is the social and commercial heart of Greek and Macedonian life in Toronto. At night, especially between Chester St and Pape Ave, lively tavernas are crowded with patrons enjoying souvlaki and seafood, accompanied by *retsina* or *ouzo*. In the day, shops are the draw *(see p83)*.

HONEY BALLS · FAMOUS BAKLAVA · CUSTARD CREAM
ALMOND COOKIES · SAMALI · FRESH DAILY BREAD

Greek shop on The Danforth

The Annex
7 This upscale neighborhood is home to students, families, and professionals. Huge trees front the Edwardian houses. Bloor St, a main traffic artery, is lined with shops between Bathurst Ave and Spadina Ave selling inexpensive clothing, jewelry, books, and secondhand CDs, and with eateries that won't tax your wallet, including many ethnic and vegetarian spots. On weekends, the streets and bars are filled with young revelers *(see p76)*.

Roncesvalles
8 Toronto's Polish community lays claim to this west-end neighborhood. Its heart, Roncesvalles Ave between Howard Park Ave and Queen St W, is lined with great Polish delis and bakeries (try the jam donuts at Granowska). Increasingly gentrifying as the ethnic population ages and moves on and young professionals move in, the area still has a working-class feel and Polish is still spoken in shops and on the street.

Leslieville
9 One of the newer areas of Toronto to take shape as a destination, what this district lacks in architectural richness it makes up for in character. Along Queen St E between Carlaw Ave and Leslie St, secondhand furniture, housewares, and vintage stores offer 1960s and 1970s bric-a-brac, though you might have to compete with the set designers from the nearby film studios for the object of your desire. Casual cafés are perfect for weekend brunches and several good restaurants have opened up here *(see p58)*. Map F4

Little India
10 The festive spirit of the market bazaars of the Indian subcontinent is alive and well – even during Toronto's cold winter – on Gerrard St E between Greenwood Ave and Coxwell Ave. Shops sell colorful saris, street vendors cook up tantalizing takeaway, and restaurants serve excellent Indian fare, from vegetarian *masala dosa* to *halwa*, a carrot-based sweet.

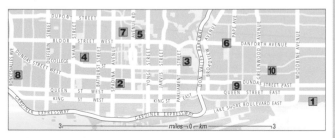

Toronto Necropolis and Crematorium, dating from the 1850s, is one of the highlights of a walk through Cabbagetown See p85

Left **Leslie Street Spit** Right **High Park**

TOP 10 Greenspaces

1 Leslie Street Spit

Officially called Outer Harbour East Headland and also known as Tommy Thompson Park – after Toronto's first commissioner of parks and the official who peppered them with "Please Walk on the Grass" signs. The northern half, designated as a nature reserve, is a man-made peninsula extending 3 miles (5 km) into Lake Ontario. More than 290 bird species have been observed here, and its wetlands, meadows, and forests contain many rare plants. The lighthouse at the southern tip is a common destination for bicyclists. ⊗ *Map F6*

2 Evergreen Brick Works

Nature and a city park have reclaimed the quarry of this historic former brickworks: the ponds and meadows of what is now known as Weston Quarry Gardens attract birds and wildlife. Stop by the world-famous excavated "wall" to see the fossils of Toronto's early flora and fauna and the region's geologic history; some of the layers of deposits are over one million years old *(see p85).*

3 High Park

Several miles of bicycle and walking trails meander through formal gardens, wooded ravines, and a rare oak savanna habitat in downtown's largest park. At the south end is Colborne Lodge *(see p92)* and Grenadier Pond, where locals fish in summer and skate in winter *(see p94).*

4 Ashbridges Bay Park

Enjoy a picnic at this lakeside park while watching boats moor, or play a game at the rugby pitch or baseball diamond. At the north end, the Martin Goodman bicycle trail *(see p94)* meets The Beach boardwalk *(see p38).*

5 Mount Pleasant Cemetery

The array of trees – many magnificently old and stately – in this cemetery dating from 1876 qualifies it as a bona fide arboretum. A walk through the lovely grounds will reveal the graves of several notable Canadians, including pianist Glenn Gould (1932–82), whose marker is carved with the opening bars of J. S. Bach's *Goldberg Variations.* ⊗ *Map D1*

Beach at Ashbridges Bay Park

Enjoy a Shakespeare play under the stars on the grassy slopes of High Park's amphitheater (Jul–Aug); call CanStage at 416 367 8243

Yorkville Park

Rouge National Urban Park
One of the largest North American parks in an urban area – over 31 sq miles (50 sq km) – borders the Rouge River and its tributaries at the city's eastern edge. In 2011 the park was designated a National Urban Park, the first of its kind in Canada. Home to a unique diversity of wildlife and plants, including a lakeshore marsh, you can easily spend a day exploring the trails, on foot or bicycle *(see p94)*.

Edwards Gardens
Marvelous flowerbeds showcasing roses, rhododendrons, and more make this formal oasis very popular in summer, especially for wedding parties. The Teaching Garden lets kids learn hands-on about nature. The Toronto Botanical Garden, a horticultural center, is also here *(see p94)*.

Yorkville Park
This gem packs a lot of punch within its compact borders. It is elegantly divided into a series of gardens, each with a different theme, such as aspen grove, wetland, and meadow. Jets of mist rise at intervals around conifers; the enormous chunk of Canadian Shield granite makes a perfect perch for a rest. ◈ *Map C3*

Humber Bay Park East
Views of the city don't get much better than those from here. Easily accessible by bicycle on the Waterfront Trail, the park is also great for exploring on foot. Major habitat restoration such as wildflower meadow plantings attracts birds and butterflies *(see p94)*. Walkways and interpretive signs complement a series of interesting stormwater cleansing ponds. ◈ *Map A2*

Toronto Music Garden
One of the city's most unusual gardens, each of its six sections is inspired by a movement in J. S. Bach's *First Suite for Unaccompanied Cello.* The swirling paths, undulating hills, and secretive groves are dazzling *(see p65)*.

Edwards Gardens

Left **Young swimmers at a public pool** Right **In-line skating on the Martin Goodman Trail**

Outdoor Activities

Swimming
Cherry Beach in the east and clothing-optional Hanlan's Point on Toronto Islands *(see p15)* are two of Toronto's best beaches. Many beaches have been awarded Blue Flags. Expect beach closures following rain storms. More reliable are the public pools. *Beaches hotline: 416 392 7161 • Beach and pool info: www.toronto.ca*

Skating
Among Toronto's 49 free outdoor rinks are Nathan Phillips Square *(see p75)* and Harbourfront Centre's Natrel Rink *(see p63)*. Both have skate rentals. *City-run rinks: 311 • Natrel Rink: 416 973 4000*

Cyclist

In-Line Skating
Daring in-line skaters take to the streets, but recreational rollers head to the lake-hugging Martin Goodman Trail *(see p94)*.

Jogging
Extensive park and ravine trails mean lots of choice. Head to the Beach boardwalk *(see p38)*, High Park *(see p40)*, or the more secluded paths by the Don River.

Cycling
Many major roads and parks have bike lanes. A terrific recreational cycle is on the Martin Goodman Trail *(see p94)* or at Leslie Street Spit *(see p40)*.

Hiking
Toronto Field Naturalists (TFN) offer daily tours of natural areas. The 500-mile (800-km) Bruce Trail, running along the Niagara Escarpment from Niagara to Tobermory, has many access points. The Bruce Trail Conservancy (BTC) is a mine of information. *TFN: 416 593 2656, www.torontofieldnaturalists.org • BTC: 1 800 665 4453, www.brucetrail.org*

Sailing on Toronto Harbour

You can rent in-line skates and bicycles from Wheel Excitement, at 249 Queens Quay W, Unit 106 (416 260 9000)

Skating at Nathan Phillips Square, City Hall

Top 10 Spectator Sports

Toronto Maple Leafs
This NHL team inspires hometown adoration. ◈ Air Canada Centre, 40 Bay St • 416 703 5323

Toronto Blue Jays
Member of Major League baseball's American League. ◈ Rogers Centre, 1 Blue Jays Way • 416 341 1234, 1-888-OK-GO-JAY

Toronto Raptors
NBA team that delights fans from November to May. ◈ Air Canada Centre, 40 Bay St • 416 366 3865

Toronto Argonauts
Canadian Football League team. ◈ Rogers Centre, 1 Blue Jays Way • 416 341 2746

Toronto Rock
Players of lacrosse, the country's official national sport. ◈ Air Canada Centre, 40 Bay St • 416 596 3075

Toronto FC
The city's Major League Soccer team. ◈ BMO Field, Exhibition Place • 416 360 4625

Woodbine Race Track
Home of the Queen's Plate horse race. ◈ 555 Rexdale Blvd • 416 675 7223

Honda Indy
Canadian highlight of the IZOD Indy Car racing series draws crowds to Exhibition Place. ◈ 416 588 7223

Scotiabank Toronto Waterfront Marathon
Boston Marathon qualifier along the shore and through the Don Valley. ◈ 416 944 2765

Toronto Marlies
The AHL team sends players to the NHL. ◈ Ricoh Coliseum, Exhibition Grounds • 416 597 7825

Windsurfing and Sailing
You can take windsurfing lessons or rent a board by joining the Toronto Windsurfing Club at Cherry Beach, the city's best surfing spot. Sailors can choose from four public marinas – the largest at Bluffer's Park (see p94) – or a number of private ones. ◈ Toronto Windsurfing Club: 416 461 7078 • Bluffer's Park Marina: 416 266 4556

Canoeing and Kayaking
The Toronto Islands' lagoons are ideal for paddling; rent a canoe on Centre Island or the mainland at Harbourfront Canoe & Kayak Centre, which also offers one-evening classes and local outings. ◈ Harbourfront Canoe & Kayak Centre: 283A Queens Quay W • 416 203 2277

Golfing
The famous Glen Abbey is just 30 minutes west of Toronto; there are also five golf courses in the city. ◈ Glen Abbey: 1333 Dorval Dr, Oakville; 905 844 1811 • Tam O'Shanter Golf Course: 416 392 2547

Skiing
Within city limits, at North York Ski Centre and Centennial Park, there are only small hills; two hours north of Toronto, at Collingwood, is Ontario's best skiing (see p98). Phone the city's information line for details. ◈ 311

To check on the water quality at any of Toronto's 14 beaches, visit the website www.toronto.ca

Left **Molson Amphitheatre** Right **The Sony Centre**

Entertainment Venues

Molson Amphitheatre

With its lakeside setting, this is a great place to take in a summer concert. There's seating for 8,000 under the copper canopy, plus space for 8,000 on the grass. Next door, Echo Beach is a smaller open-air venue with no reserved seating. *909 Lake Shore Blvd W • Map A5 • 416 260 5600 • www.canadian amphitheatre.net*

Roy Thomson Hall

The concert hall's innovative design ensures that everyone in the audience is within 100 ft (30 m) of the stage *(see p13)*. It is home to the Toronto Symphony Orchestra (perform September to June) and Toronto Mendelssohn Choir, and also hosts many guest artists. *60 Simcoe St • Map J4 • 416 872 4255 • www.roythomson.com*

Roy Thomson Hall

St. Lawrence Centre for the Arts

This venerable Toronto venue presents theater, dance, and music, along with lectures on subjects of topical interest, in its two intimate spaces. The Canadian Stage Theatre Company is based in the larger Bluma Appel Theatre, while Jane Mallet Theatre features recitals and performances by groups such as the Toronto Operetta Theatre Company. *27 Front St E • Map L5 • 416 366 7723 • www.stlc.com*

The Sony Centre

It was here that famed dancer Mikhail Baryshnikov defected from the Soviet Union in 1979. The now refurbished theater mounts shows as diverse as Beck, Sesame Street Live, and the Eifman St Petersburg Ballet. *1 Front St E • Map L5 • 1 855 872 7669 • www.sonycentre.ca*

Koerner Hall

Part of the Royal Conservatory of Music's Telus Centre for Performing and Learning, Koerner Hall's acoustics are second to none. Enjoy classical, jazz, and World Music here. *273 Bloor St W • Map C3 • 416 408 0208 • www.performance.rcmusica.ca*

Young Centre for the Performing Arts

Home of the respected Soulpepper Theatre Company, this performance space is also the main venue for the George Brown Theatre School and hosts a number of other local performances. *50 Tank House Lane • Map E5 • 416 866 8666 • www.youngcentre.ca*

Koerner Hall

For events listings, check out NOW magazine See p110

Winter Garden Theatre

Elgin and Winter Garden Theatres

These two theaters have been restored to their original splendor. Opened in 1913 as a double-decker venue – the Winter Garden seven stories above the Elgin – they host concerts, operas, and hit Broadway musicals *(see p68)*.

Massey Hall

This grand dame of entertainment venues, opened in 1894, was the first dedicated music hall in Toronto with the stage space to accommodate large musical groups. Its 2,750 seats and superb acoustics provide a surprisingly intimate setting for jazz, blues, and folk shows. ⊗ *178 Victoria St • Map L4 • 416 872 4255 • www.masseyhall.com*

Four Seasons Centre for the Performing Arts

A large, beautiful space, the Four Seasons is home to two of Canada's most important performing arts companies – the National Ballet of Canada and the Canadian Opera Company. ⊗ *145 Queen St W • Map K4 • COC: 416 363 8231, www. coc.ca • NBC: 416 345 9595, www. national.ballet.ca*

Glenn Gould Studio

CBC, Canada's national broadcaster, records for-radio musical performances, from classical to jazz, in this small studio named after the famous concert pianist. ⊗ *250 Front St W • Map J5 • 416 205 5555 • www.cbc.ca/glenngould*

Top 10 Performing Arts Groups

1 Canadian Opera Company

The COC is the largest producer of opera in Canada and stages seven productions each season.

2 Tarragon Theatre

New innovative works by Canadian playwrights.

3 Tafelmusik

The ensemble plays Baroque chamber music on period instruments.

4 Theatre Passe Muraille

This pioneering theater is instrumental in shaping a distinctly Canadian voice.

5 Toronto Mendelssohn Choir

Canada's oldest vocal ensemble presented its first concert in 1895.

6 Toronto Symphony Orchestra

This world-renowned orchestra delights audiences with the classics.

7 Canadian Stage Company

Theatrical productions of international and Canadian works, including musicals.

8 National Ballet of Canada

Internationally acclaimed company dances the classics with luster, and presents vibrant new choreography.

9 Toronto Dance Theatre

Intelligent and visually striking modern dance by one of the country's most influential dance troupes.

10 Soulpepper Theatre Company

Canadian interpretations of international classics.

 The Rogers Centre **(See p63)** *and the Air Canada Centre* **(See p66)** *play host to big name musicians; visit www.heritagetrust.on.ca/EWG*

Left **Fans vying for autographs at TIFF** Right **People parading in Pride Week**

Festivals

Luminato
This internationally acclaimed multi-arts festival takes place over ten days and brings out the cutting-edge big hitters – think actress Isabella Rossellini dressed like a bunny and artist Matthew Barney's six-hour film premieres. There's music galore, both international and local, plus dance, and talks by the likes of musicians David Byrne, Joni Mitchell, and Buffy Sainte Marie. Also many free events and even some stuff for kids. ◎ *Jun • www.luminatofestival.com*

NXNE
Begun as a grungy music event, North By Northeast has grown almost as momentously as Austin Texas's SXSW. Now a cultural extravaganza encompassing film, art, talks, and new technology, NXNE takes over the downtown core for ten days. Get your wrist band and get out there – it's still an unbeatable chance to discover new bands. ◎ *Jun • www.nxne.com*

Carnival costume

TIFF
For ten days in early September, Toronto rolls out the red carpet to cinema's greatest. Showcasing over 300 films from as many as 60 countries, the Toronto International Film Festival draws stars, independent film makers, and movie buffs to the city. Luxury hotels fill up and the festival HQ TIFF Bell Lightbox at John and King becomes a hive of activity. ◎ *Sep • www.tiff.net*

Nuit Blanche
An all night contemporary arts festival, with over 100 art events scattered across town. Stay up until dawn – it can get pretty interesting. ◎ *Early Oct • www.scotiabanknuitblanche.com*

Caribbean Carnival
A three-week extravaganza celebrating all things Caribbean, especially the music, including Soca, steel pan, reggae, hip hop, and more. The revelry culminates on the August long weekend with a huge parade, packed with elaborate costumes, along Lakeshore Blvd. ◎ *Jul to early Aug • www.torontocaribbeancarnival.com*

Contact
The largest festival dedicated to photography in the world, Contact brings over 1,500 artists to exhibit at 175 venues in the city. Big names round out the program along with retrospectives of the greats. ◎ *May • www.scotiabankcontactphoto.com*

For details on Toronto International Film Festival, call 416 968 3456 or visit the box office at 2 Carlton St W, mezzanine level

A screening during Hot Docs

SummerWorks

This ten-day festival of performance is run by Summer-Works, known for its quality, forward-thinking Canadian theater. It is the biggest juried festival in Canada. ⊗ Aug • www.summer works.ca

Pride Week

Toronto's Pride celebrations are legendary. Performances, music, and parties take over the Village around Church and Wellesley for ten days. Three parades make sure all are repre-sented – the Dyke March, Trans Parade, and the fabulously fun Pride Parade. ⊗ late Jun
• www.pridetoronto.com

Beaches International Jazz Festival

For a completely free festival, Beaches packs a real punch, with mostly Canadian headliners, a Big Band Stage, and a Latino Stage. Over 40 bands play along Queen St East and the crowds bring the neighborhood to a standstill. ⊗ Late Jul • www.beaches-jazz.com

Hot Docs

An 11-day festival dedicated to the art of documentary film making, with around 200 films from Canada and around the world screened in 16 venues across the city. ⊗ late Apr
• www.hotdocs.ca

Top 10 Family Events

1 Canadian National Exhibition
Themed pavilions, fairground amusements, and an air show. ⊗ mid-Aug to Labour Day
• www.theex.com

2 Canada Day
Free concerts, activities, and fireworks at Mel Lastman Square. ⊗ Jul 1st

3 TIFF Kids
The best in contemporary and classic children's film.
⊗ Apr • www.tiff.net

4 Santa Claus Parade
Toronto tradition featuring floats, marching bands, and the big man himself. ⊗ mid-Nov
• www.thesantaclausparade.ca

5 Royal Agricultural Winter Fair
Country fair with horse jump-ing and livestock competitions.
⊗ Nov • www.royalfair.org

6 Buskerfest
Acrobats, musicians, and more take over Yonge between Queen and College. ⊗ late Aug
• www.torontobuskerfest.com

7 Dragon Boat Race Festival
Teams from around the world compete in a race at Centre Island. ⊗ Jun • www.dragon boats.com

8 Redpath Waterfront Festival
Fun along the shore, with treasure hunts, a flyboarding competition, and dog trials. ⊗ Jun • www.towaterfrontfest.com

9 Sugarbush Maple Syrup Festival
Learn how to make maple syrup. ⊗ Mar–Apr • www. maplesyrupfest.com

10 Word on the Street
Literary festival with read-ings by popular authors. ⊗ Sep
• www.thewordonthestreet.ca

Left **Royal Ontario Museum** Right **Ontario Science Centre**

🔟 Children's Attractions

Royal Ontario Museum
A truly magical place for children, Canada's largest museum makes a special effort to have plenty of hands-on exhibits. The Dinosaur Gallery and mummy cases are strictly "don't touch," but the Hands-On Biodiversity Gallery enchants youngsters with interactive exhibits, as does the CIBC Discovery Room *(see pp8–11)*.

Hockey Hall of Fame
Budding hockey stars can test their skill whacking pucks and guarding goal at this shrine to the sport, which houses more hockey memorabilia than you can shake a stick at *(see pp26–7)*.

Hockey Hall of Fame logo

Ripley's Aquarium of Canada
Kids will love the tanks filled with all things marine, especially those with perspex bubbles and tunnels they can crawl into to be part of the display *(see pp22–3)*.

Toronto Zoo
Exhibiting animals in their natural habitats is the policy of this zoo, which aims for meaningful education over theme-park spectacle. Six geographic areas are represented in pavilions filled with over 500 species; large outdoor enclosures allow animals to roam freely *(see p91)*.

Ontario Science Centre
No need to reign in the kids at this science-based learning playground. Instead, let them charge through the more than 800 hands-on exhibits encompassing everything from sports to medicine, computers to electricity *(see p91)*.

Riverdale Farm
This agricultural education center and working farm in the middle of the city is home to many barnyard favorites – pigs, goats, sheep, horses, and chickens. Post-and-beam barns date from the 19th century. This is a re-creation of a working farm, and animals should not be petted. 🌾 *201 Winchester St • Map E3 • Open 9am–5pm daily*

Toronto Zoo

SkyRider, Canada's Wonderland

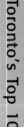

Canada's Wonderland

7 This amusement park north of the city has 200 attractions, including over 65 rides, a water park, and live shows. Thrill rides for older kids, tamer rides for little ones. ✪ 9580 Jane St, Vaughan • Map A1 • Open May–Sep; hrs vary, call 905 832 8131 • Adm • www.canadas wonderland.com

Harbourfront

8 The kid-friendly attractions and events at this lakefront center ensure it's always busy. Kids especially love watching artisans at work in the Artport's Craft Studio, the ice-skating rink *(see p42)*, and open-air concerts.

Young People's Theatre

9 This theater presents excellent productions that are always a hit with children. The façade of the original building, built in 1881 as a stable for street-car-pulling horses, can still be seen. ✪ 165 Front St E • Map M4 • 416 862 2222 • www.youngpeoplestheatre.ca

Centre Island

10 A highlight of this Toronto island is Centreville, a bustling amusement park. Some 30 old-fashioned rides include "swan" paddle boats, a 1907 carousel, and pony rides *(see p15)*.

Top 10 Places to Eat with Kids

1 Sunset Grill
Kids love diners and this is a particularly good one located in The Beach. ✪ 2006 Queen St E • 416 690 9985

2 Wayne Gretzky's
Pub fare, a kids' menu, and, of course, a hockey memorabilia decor. ✪ 99 Blue Jays Way • Map J4 • 416 979 7825

3 Five Doors North
Classic Italian pastas and grilled meats; desserts come in heroic portions. ✪ 2088 Yonge St • Map B2 • 416 480 6234

4 Swiss Chalet
Canadian chain stuck in the 1980s, but reliably kid pleasing. Good rotisserie chicken. ✪ 266 Queens Quay W • Map J6 • 416 596 7292

5 Grano
Upscale but kid-friendly restaurant with fantastic Italian food. ✪ 2035 Yonge St • Map B2 • 416 440 1986

6 Magic Oven
Delicious pizza and pasta just east of Pape. ✪ 798 Danforth Ave • Map F3 • 416 868 6836

7 Mr. Greenjeans
Burgers and hot dogs for the kids, served with fun and flair. ✪ Eaton Centre • Map L3 • 416 979 1212

8 Lee Garden
Lively dining room and oodles of noodles. A long-time favorite *(see p81)*.

9 Hero Certified Burger
Local burger chain with food that beats international fast-food eateries. ✪ 441 Queen St W • Map H4 • 416 581 1149

10 Old Spaghetti Factory
A perennial favorite, great for groups. ✪ 54 The Esplanade • Map L5 • 416 864 9761

Left **Church Street** Right **AIDS Memorial, Cawthra Square Park**

🔟 Gay & Lesbian Hangouts

Church Street
The intersection of Church and Wellesley Streets, the epicenter of Toronto's gay village, has been home to a large gay and lesbian community for decades. A profusion of excellent bars, restaurants, and specialty shops make the strip a great place to just hang out and soak up the scene as leathermen, muscle boys, and drag queens strut their stuff. The 519 Community Centre at 519 Church Street hosts regular social events and neighborhood gatherings, as well as offering a multitude of drop-in programs and short-term counseling. ⊗ *Map L1*

Buddies

Club 120
Located on two floors above a restaurant on the Church St/ Richmond St intersection, this upscale nightclub hosts a plethora of events including T-Girl nights, open-mic comedy nights, and a monthly naked dance party TNT!MEN. On the weekends the crowds mix up and things really get going with international DJs holding court late into the night. Check the website for the events schedule. ⊗ *120 Church St • Map L4 • www.club120.ca*

Cawthra Square Park
This popular meeting place, with its benches and greenery, is home to a permanent AIDS memorial, installed in 1993. The pillars are inscribed, upon request and with no geographic restrictions, with the names of people lost to the disease. The Universal Remembrance Plaque, added in 1995, is a tribute to those who remain unnamed. ⊗ *South of 519 Church St • Map L1*

Crews & Tangos
A fabulous fun spot to dance the night away on two separate dance floors – hip hop, R&B, top 40, and the best local and NY-based DJs around. Once a girl bar, now the welcoming crowd is mixed. If you are after some theatricality you've come to the right place – there's a drag show every night. ⊗ *508 Church St • Map L1 • 637 349 7469*

Glad Day Bookshop
Established in 1970 as Canada's first gay and lesbian bookstore, its excellent collection includes a wide selection of academic, fiction, and hard-to-find titles, as well as racy picture

Glad Day Bookshop

Annual Pride Week events (late Jun) include performances, a Dyke March, and the Pride Parade; visit www.pridetoronto.com for details

books and magazines. The used books section on the second floor is definitely worth checking out. ⊗ 598A Yonge St • Map L1 • 416 961 4161

Woody's
A stuffed rhinoceros head presiding over the bar greets patrons at this local watering hole. A pool table and continuously running soft-core videos keep the clientele entertained, as do special events, like the popular Best Chest contest, here and at sibling bar Sailor, next door. ⊗ 467 Church St • Map L1 • 416 972 0887

Hair of the Dog
This laid-back spot serves standard pub fare alongside draft beer. The sizeable patio is the big draw here, located at the back and south facing. ⊗ 425 Church St • Map L2 • 416 964 2708

Buddies in Bad Times Theatre
This groundbreaking theater company, established in 1979, is the city's oldest and largest venue for queer-culture productions. Renowned for innovative, edgy works, productions often push the boundaries of artistic convention and sometimes even propriety – but that's precisely the point. On Saturdays at 10:30pm Tallulah's Cabaret takes over with DJs and wild dancing and, true to its name, some kind of outrageous performance. There's plenty of information on Tallulah's Cabaret nights, plus upcoming festivals and events, on the theater's website where you can also buy tickets. ⊗ 12 Alexander St • Map L1 • 416 975 8555 • www.bud diesinbadtimes.com

Woody's and Sailor

The Beaver
Head west to this laid-back little café that turns into raucous fun from 11pm, featuring DJs that spin hip hop, dancehall, 1990s grunge, and even country. On Sundays there's karaoke and once a month join in Punk Rock Bingo at 9pm. ⊗ 1192 Queen St W • Map A4 • 416 537 2768

Hanlan's Point Beach
This secluded Toronto Island beach has the city's only official clothing-optional area. (Don't take off your clothes until you reach the well-signed, fenced section at the south end.) In 1999, the Point reclaimed its status as a nude beach, as it had been between 1894 and 1930, enabling nudists and cruisers to again bathe in the buff. There are "no swimming" signs when water pollution levels are high (see p15). ⊗ Map B6

The Village is fun but if it's not quite your scene, a more alternative vibe can be found at a sprinkling of bars west of downtown in Parkdale

51

Left **The Chase** Right **Canoe**

Restaurants

Splendido
Swoon over upscale Canadian cuisine at this respected eatery. The creative chefs employ high-end indulgences such as black truffles, Quebecoise fois gras, and smoked oysters with staggering effect. The kitchen has done most of the thinking for you – choose between the five course set meal or the seemingly endless tasting menu. Open for dinner only. ✆ 88 Harbord St • Map C3 • 416 929 7788 • $$$$$

The Fifth Grill
This steak house with a distinct French influence styles itself as a club (and yes, non-members do pay slightly more); the freight-elevator ride to the fifth floor loft only adds to the exclusive feel of the place. In winter, candles, fireplace, and couches make things lavishly cozy. In summer, try for a table on the rooftop terrace. ✆ 225 Richmond St W • Map J4 • 416 979 3005 • www.thefifthgrill.com • $$$$$

Splendido

Canoe
Stellar views from the 54th floor of the Toronto Dominion Bank Tower make this one of the most enchanting rooms in the city. Lunchtime business crowds may close deals over lobster club-house sandwiches on brioche, but the evening ambience is much more romantic. Menu mainstays include Canadian elk and Quebec suckling pig (see p69).

Starfish's catch of the day

Starfish
This low-key, sophisticated restaurant specializes in fish and seafood. Come here for the oysters, which hale from Canada's East Coast and Ireland's Galway Bay. Pair them with local wines or a pint of stout. And for afters, the sticky toffee pudding is unbeatable ✆ 100 Adelaide St East • Map M4 • 416 366-7827 • $$$

The Chase
Refined dining in a bright, window-walled penthouse atop the Heritage listed Dineen Building. Carefully prepared dishes, such as lobster layered with truffles, rack of lamb with millet *arincini*, or chestnut and foie gras ravioli, allow the world-class surf-n-turf to sing. Less formal dining in The Chase Fish and Oyster on the ground floor. ✆ 10 Temperance St • Map L4 • 647 348 7000 • $$$$$

Chiado

Lai Wah Heen

With exceptional Cantonese cuisine, this elegant two-level restaurant in the DoubleTree by Hilton redefines and updates classic Chinese fare. Haute details include silver chopstick rests and starched linens on the round tables, which are suitable for large groups and conducive to sharing (smaller tables also available). Sunday dim sum is particularly popular. ⓢ *108 Chestnut St • Map K3 • 416 977 9899 • $$$$*

Chiado

Dine on the freshest fish and seafood to be had in the city, flown in from the world's wharfs daily and transformed into the most luxurious of Portuguese fare. The wine list is replete with unusual offerings which the waitstaff are expert at elucidating and pairing with dishes. Try the tapas menu at the wine bar in the restaurant's modern annex addition, Senhor Antonio. ⓢ *864 College St • Map A3 • 416 538 1910 • $$$$$*

Sushi Kaji

Masterful chef Mitsuhiro Kaji creates the city's premiere Japanese cuisine with ingredients flown in from Japan. The restaurant has two private rooms, but it is great to perch at the eight-seat sushi bar to enjoy the food-as-theater experience. Premium sakes are the perfect accompaniment to excellent – and generously portioned – sushi, sashimi, and creative cooked offerings *(see p95)*.

Noce

This intimate restaurant serves marvelous Italian food, delivered with welcoming, friendly service. The home-made pasta specials are always superb, as are grilled and roasted meats. The summer patio is great for al fresco dining. ⓢ *875 Queen St W • Map B4 • 416 504 3463 • $$$$*

Buca

This trendy basement *osteria* is tucked up an alley way that runs beside the Scholastic building just west of Portland Street. The acclaimed, earthy Italian fare includes unusual quirks like bison prosciutto. Delicious *nodini* (garlic ball rolls), too. ⓢ *604 King St W • Map G4 • 416 865 1600 • $$$$*

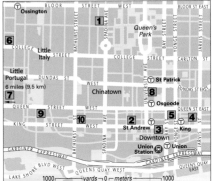

Left **Gallery Grill** Right **Lakeview Lunch**

Brunches

Le Sélect Bistro
A much-loved Toronto mainstay serving all the popular weekend brunch options as well as Alsace classics like *choucroute* and *confit du canard* (see p69).

Lakeview Lunch
Slide into a booth – part of the old-style diner decor – and choose from a menu that focuses on eggs and burger classics. Good milkshakes 24/7. ◐ 1132 Dundas St W • Map A4 • 416 535 2828 • $

Courtyard Café
This elegant restaurant in the venerable Windsor Arms Hotel has for decades been a city favorite for a romantic Sunday brunch. The traditional-style buffet includes salmon, made-to-order omelets, roasts, and desserts. ◐ 18 St Thomas St • Map C3 • 416 921 2921 • $$$$

Courtyard Café

Bonjour Brioche
This bakery-cum-café is popular with locals, so arrive early to get a seat. Brioches and croissants (in several flavors) are baked on the premises and melt-in-your-mouth fresh. Sandwiches on chewy baguettes are excellent. ◐ 812 Queen St E • Map F4 • 416 406 1250 • $

Fruit tart, Bonjour Brioche

Gallery Grill
The Neo-Gothic splendor of the University of Toronto's Hart House sets the tone of refined tradition, and the menu adds sparkle to the sedate surroundings. Classy choices to go with your eggs include smoked trout and fried green tomatoes or pancetta-Roquefort *tart flambé*. Serves brunch on Sundays. ◐ 7 Hart House Circle • Map J1 • 416 978 2445 • Closed Sat • $$$

Lady Marmalade
Among the best places for brunch in breakfast-crazy Leslieville. Mexican-inspired *huevos* and creative takes on eggs benedict. ◐ 898 Queen St E • Map F4 • 647 351 7645 • $

One
Star chef Mark McEwan's glamorous eatery is located in the upscale Hazelton Hotel. Spend a lazy morning celeb-spotting while grazing on a wide choice of breakfast options.

Alternatively, go for a classy cocktail before choosing from the extensive dinner menu. Brunch is served on weekends from 10:30am to 4:30pm. ✆ *116 Yorkville Ave • Map C3 • 416 961 9600 • $$$$*

Mildred's Temple Kitchen
Set in a post-industrial district of Victorian-era, brick factories, Mildred's features a farmhouse chic menu of dishes created with seasonal produce. On weekends try the Big Brunch Skillet of pulled pork, black beans, and eggs, or Veda's Choice – eggs benedict on a croissant. The rosemary bacon is cured in-house. ✆ *85 Hanna Ave • Map A5 • 416 588 5695 • $$*

Aunties and Uncles
A charmingly eclectic eatery in a former 1950s barber shop. Soups, salads, omelets, and sandwiches are excellent, the juice freshly squeezed. ✆ *74 Lippincott St • Map B3 • 416 324 1375 • $*

Counter seating at Swan

Swan
A Formica-topped counter and reclaimed diner booths lend this classy spot a 1950s feel, but the food is decidedly contemporary. Eggs are scrambled with smoked oysters and pancetta, sautéed spinach accompanies trout eggs benny. Excellent Americano coffee, but alas, no free refills. ✆ *892 Queen St W • Map B4 • 416 532 0452 • $$*

Top 10 Best Snacks

Chinese Buns
Steamed dough filled with savory meat, vegetables, or sweet coconut and red bean paste. Eat piping hot.

Poutine
Hailing from Québec, *poutine* (french fries topped with cheese curds and hot gravy), is now ubiquitous in Toronto.

Falafel
Deep-fried chickpea balls in pita pockets stuffed with *tahini* sauce, onion, and tomato – a Lebanese specialty.

Bubble Tea
An Asian concoction of sweet, flavored cold tea, milk, and tapioca pearls.

Gelato
More refreshing and lighter than ice cream, Italian ices come in an assortment of flavors, from lemon to caramel.

Corn on the Cob
Little India street vendors prepare grilled corn glazed with lemon juice and spices.

Hot Dogs
Ubiquitous outdoor carts grill hot dogs, veggie dogs, and sausages. Polish sausage is a favorite, piled high with all the fixings – pickles, sauerkraut, and hot mustard.

Jamaican Roti
Soft flat bread encases a variety of fillings, from curried goat or chicken to spinach and squash. Hot sauce is optional.

Churrasco Chicken
Spiked with tangy Portuguese *piri piri* sauce, then barbecued to perfection; served on a bun or with roasted spuds.

Roasted Chestnuts
Sidewalk vendors sell steaming-hot smoky-flavored chestnuts in summer and fall.

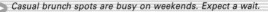

Left **dBar** Right **The Roof Lounge**

🔟 **Bars & Clubs**

1 Crush
Just as diners are ordering dessert, the lights are dimmed and the music turned up, officially ushering in the night to this restaurant and wine bar. A terrific selection of wines, many by the glass and fairly priced. The splendid loft space has a large adjoining patio *(see p67)*.

2 The Roof Lounge
A haunt of creative types, this bar atop the Park Hyatt Hotel offers refuge from daily stresses. In winter, a fireplace and huge leather chairs beckon; in summer, spectacular views from the terrace *(see p80)*.

Cameron House ant sculpture

3 Bar Hop
The bars that sold proper cask-pulled beer were few and far between a decade ago. Finally, Toronto has at last joined the craft beer renaissance, serving pints from microbreweries scattered across Ontario. Bar Hop is among the best of the new breed, bringing in guest beers regularly to join its 36 taps *(see p67)*.

4 dBar
It's all about style at this busy see-and-be-seen bar on the ground floor of the prestigious Four Seasons Hotel in fashionable Yorkville. At your table, adept servers prepare the perfect cocktail in a miniature shaker; nary a drop is spilled. At the bar, business tycoons talk takeovers while scoping out the room *(see p80)*.

5 Cameron House
Giant "ants" on the front of this former flophouse signal a different bar experience. Unspoiled by the acts that played here before making it big, this low-key bar is dedicated to up-and-coming musicians. Join foot-stomping regulars on weekend evenings for pay-what-you-can country music *(see p80)*.

6 Pravda Vodka House
Decked out in gold and Russian red furnishings, with portraits of Stalin and Lenin on the walls, this bar serves up more than 70 of the world's best vodkas *(see p88)*.

Crush

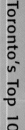

Irish Embassy Pub & Grill

Top Ten Places to See Live Music

1 Opera House
An eclectic range of bands plays beneath the ornate proscenium arch. All-ages shows and blues nights pack the place. ✆ 735 Queen St E • Map F4

2 Rivoli
Booking top alternative rock bands has made this spot a Toronto landmark. ✆ 334 Queen St W • Map H4

3 Danforth Music Hall
Originally a cinema, this mid-size venue has a balcony and slanted floors. ✆ 147 Danforth Ave • Map F3

4 Horseshoe Tavern
A stalwart of Queen West since 1947 showcasing the best of Toronto bands. ✆ 368 Queen St W • Map H4

5 Adelaide Hall
Great intimate venue for indie bands and other acts, right in the heart of the city. ✆ 250 Adelaide St W • Map J4

6 The Rex Hotel
The hotel's jazz and blues bar attracts Canada's finest musicians. ✆ 194 Queen St W • Map J3

7 Hugh's Room
Enjoy a range of musical genres in an intimate space. ✆ 2261 Dundas St W • Map A4

8 Lee's Palace
This gritty joint hosts edgy rock bands. ✆ 529 Bloor St W • Map B3

9 Reservoir Lounge
Swing-jazz and jump blues; southern fusion cuisine. ✆ 52 Wellington St E • Map L4 • Closed Sun

10 Phoenix Concert Theatre
Rock bands, and dancing on DJ'd theme nights. ✆ 410 Sherbourne St • Map M1

7 Irish Embassy Pub & Grill
Pub lovers will feel at home with the mahogany bar and stool and booth seating set among the marble columns of this historic bank building. Good choice of beers on tap, and tasty pub food, including sirloin burgers *(see p88)*.

8 The Fifth Social Club
The loft-style dance club of this restaurant/bar venue *(see p52)* caters to the 25-plus crowd. Bouncers ignore the jeans-clad in favor of those casual-smart; once inside, grab a drink at one of four bars, then dance to R&B and top-40 music or go private in an over-sized, bottle-service VIP section *(see p67)*.

9 Lula Lounge
Lively bands and hot DJs play everything Latin, from salsa to merengue. Enjoy dinner before the show, arrive later for drinks, or go all out with a dance lesson-dinner-show package *(see p80)*.

10 Bar at Canoe
On the 54th floor of the TD Bank Tower *(see p64)*, this sophisticated spot caters to corporate wheelers and dealers (reduced to size against the magnificent view of Lake Ontario). Excellent wines, cocktails, and beer selection. Note that the bar is closed on weekends *(see p67)*.

Toronto's Top 10

Most live music venues are licensed bars and entrance is limited to those 19 years and older, unless an event is specifically all-ages

Left **Street sign, West Queen West** Right **Fresh fish, Chinatown**

🔟 Shopping Destinations

1 West Queen West
For independent designs and trendy togs, Queen West of Bathurst is the place to head. You'll find great shoe shops with the latest off-the-wall designs, slick homewares, one-of-a-kind boutiques, and cafés galore. A flurry of cool international outlets has cropped up around Ossington, including Fred Perry and Stüssy *(see p78)*.

2 Queen Street West
Artists after cheap rent settled among the textile shops along Queen Street between University Avenue and Bathurst Street in the early 1980s. Things have changed considerably and now the strip between John St and Spadina is dominated by global brands – Gap, Lululemon, Zara and the like. If you're after sneakers, there's plenty of choice, and the Crocs flagship store is here. ✪ *Map G4–J4*

3 Kensington Market
This chaotic enclave is a true gem. Once a Jewish market, the predominant ethnic flavor is now Portuguese and West Indian, with strong hints of Asian and Hispanic.

Kensington Market

Distillery District

The many food shops reflect this, stocked as they are with cassava, cornbread, pulses, cheese, salted cod, and spices. You'll also come across gourmet butchers and delicatessen. The waft of incense and strains of Reggae will lead you to the dimly lit secondhand clothing stores, which occupy the Victorian houses on Kensington Avenue *(see p73)*.

4 Distillery District
If you're after art or unique crafts visit the cobbled lanes of the Distillery District. More and more clothes retailers, including Canadian fashion heroes Got Style and crazy cobbler John Fluevog, are moving into the area's stunning spaces. ✪ *Map E5*

5 Leslieville
Lovers of vintage clothes, radios and vinyl, and mid-20th century modern furniture – some from well-known designers – will have a shopping fest along this eclectic stretch running between Logan and Greenwood. The shops are well spread out – the greatest concentration is between Carlaw and Jones *(see p39)*.

Shop window, Yorkville

Yorkville
Clustered in this upscale district, choice boutiques and fine art galleries offer everything the well-heeled and -monied traveler desires – from designer jeans to Cuban cigars. The eclectic mix of independent shops here is a welcome relief from the rows of big brash luxury shops that line the southern edge of Yorkville *(see p77)*.

Chinatown
You may think you're in Hong Kong as you browse along Spadina Avenue and Dundas Street, speculating on the use of exotic ingredients such as dried shrimp and the odoriferous durian fruit, or eyeing the dizzying array of Chinese housewares, knick-knacks, and herbal medicines on offer. A terrific place to find unusual souvenirs at low prices *(see p73)*.

Toronto Eaton Centre
Anchored at the southern end of Queen St by The Bay, this shopping oasis has something for every taste and bank balance. Electronics, make-up, skiing equipment, fashion – the range of goods across hundreds of stores is huge *(see pp24–5)*.

St. Lawrence Market
Considered by gastronomes around the globe as one of the world's best markets, a visit here is reason enough for food lovers to travel to Toronto. A huge selection of meat, fish, cheese, and produce, as well as hand-crafted gifts, make for a one-of-a-kind experience. Vendors pushing food samples and buskers add to the dynamic atmosphere; frequent special events and festivals liven things up even more. When you can't carry another thing, visit the free parcel check on the west side of the lower level, outside *(see p86)*.

Bloor Street
Bloor Street between Yonge Street and Avenue Road grows ever more luxurious with branches of Gucci, Tiffany's, Hermès, Chanel, and Max Mara, as well as excellent homegrown stores. Drop by fine jewelers Birks; William Ashley China, a top-notch china and glass store; Holt Renfrew, a small department store specializing in high-end clothing; Harry Rosen, a superb men's clothing store with impeccable service; and the Roots flagship store, offering quality leather and sportswear *(see p77)*.

The Cumberland exit of the Bay subway stop (Bloor line) puts you right in the center of Yorkville

AROUND
TOWN

TORONTO'S TOP 10

Left **Marina at Harbourfront** Right **Bill Boyle Artport, Harbourfront Centre**

Harbourfront & the Financial District

THE STREETS OF HARBOURFRONT *and the Financial District combine old and new in a vibrant mix. Along the shores of Lake Ontario, the origins of the city can be traced to the establishment of Fort York in 1793. As the town of York grew, spreading north from the lake, financial institutions settled around Bay and King streets. Today, modern skyscrapers, interspersed with historic buildings, are dotted throughout the district, and historic vaudeville theaters, restored to their original splendor, anchor an exuberant entertainment scene.*

Sights

1. Toronto Islands
2. Queen's Quay Terminal
3. Harbourfront Centre
4. Rogers Centre
5. Toronto-Dominion Centre
6. CN Tower
7. Fort York
8. Hockey Hall of Fame
9. Ripley's Aquarium of Canada
10. Toronto Music Garden

Detail from *The Audience*, by Michael Snow, Rogers Centre

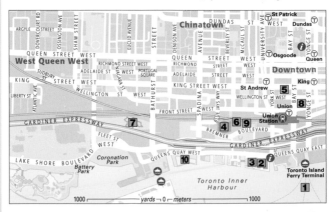

Discover more at www.dk.com

Queen's Quay Terminal

Harbourfront Centre

This cultural complex provides a diverse range of recreational and cultural activities. The Bill Boyle Artport, a converted warehouse, is the fulcrum of the centre. Watch artists shaping and blowing glass in the craft and design studios, or check out the contemporary Canadian art at the Artport Gallery. The Brigantine Room hosts a packed roster of readings and theater performances. Outside, a café overlooking the pond, which becomes a skating rink in winter *(see p42)*, serves light meals and snacks. ✆ *235 Queens Quay W • Map K6 • 416 973 4000 • Open 10am–11pm Mon–Sat, 10am–9pm Sun • www.harbourfrontcentre.com*

Toronto Islands

Recreational opportunities – from sunbathing to cycling to children's amusement rides – abound on the car-free islands, Toronto's summer playground for more than a century. Ferries depart regularly for the islands from the foot of Bay Street; the 10-minute trip across the harbor offers unparalleled views of downtown *(see pp14–15)*.

Queen's Quay Terminal

In a grand 1926 building that looks like a layered cake, this retail complex is bursting with boutiques selling unusual gift items, Native art, crafts, clothing, kitchenware, toys, and chocolates. Many restaurants, several with patios overlooking the water, offer good fare. Harbor cruises depart alongside the terminal. ✆ *207 Queens Quay W • Map K6 • 416 203 3269 • Open 10am–6pm daily*

Rogers Centre

At the base of the CN Tower, this sports and large-events venue is home to the city's baseball team, the Blue Jays, and football team, the Argonauts. When built in 1989, it had the world's only fully retractable roof of its kind, which takes just 20 minutes to open or close. When teams are not in action, you can tour the facility and peek into players' dressing rooms. Outside, on the northeast corner of the building, a frieze by Toronto artist Michael Snow depicts 14 spectators. ✆ *1 Blue Jays Way • Map J5 • 416 341 1000*

Harbourfront

5 Toronto-Dominion Centre

This six-tower complex is one of the most important pieces of architecture in the city *(see p36)*. The black steel I-beams of the 1968 Toronto Dominion Bank Tower are trademark Mies van der Rohe (1886–1969), and perfectly reflect the architect's modernist dictum that "Less is more." In the plaza, a circular bronze sculpture, Al McWilliams's *Wall and Chairs*, echoes the towers' austerity. Below ground is a shopping mall, the only one van der Rohe ever designed.
Ⓢ 55 King St W • Map K4

6 CN Tower

Soaring 1,815 ft (553 m) above downtown Toronto, this is the defining icon of the city's skyline and the tallest building in the Western Hemisphere. Before heading up, check out the state-of-the-art theater showing short but thrilling 3-D movies. Then let a glass-fronted elevator zip you, in less than a minute, to one of four

Toronto-Dominion Centre

lookout levels. Access to the SkyPod, which requires an extra fee, is by a separate elevator. The experience is vertiginous and can be rather cramped. The revolving 360 Restaurant, offers fine food in serene surroundings *(see pp12–13)*.

7 Fort York

This garrison, established by Lieutenant Governor John Graves Simcoe in 1793 to protect the growing city, was the site of the fierce Battle of York during the War of 1812, when the US invaded Upper Canada. Home to the country's largest collection of War of 1812 buildings (brick structures that replaced the fort's original wood cabins), the restored fort has fascinating displays of historic military artifacts. Guides in costume lead tours and give period music, musket, and drill demonstrations.
Ⓢ 250 Fort York Blvd • Map G5 • 416 392 6907 • Open early Sep–late May: 10am–4pm Mon–Fri, 10am–5pm Sat & Sun; late May–early Sep: 10am–5pm daily • Closed for special events • Adm

8 Hockey Hall of Fame

Hockey fans will be fascinated by the memorabilia on view at this museum dedicated to Canada's favorite sport. Everything from masks personalized by goalies to hand-carved skates from the 1840s reflect the history of the game. Have your photo taken with the iconic Stanley Cup, then test your skill at the game at the interactive exhibits *(see pp26–7)*.

Canada's War Against the US

On June 18, 1812, the US declared war on Great Britain and, for months, battled at various border outposts such as Detroit and Queenston Heights. In April 1813, American troops invaded York (as Toronto was then called), occupying the town, burning the Parliament buildings, and destroying much of Fort York. Although the US won the Battle of York, they soon abandoned the town to fight battles in the Niagara Peninsula, with mixed results. The American war with Britain ended in stalemate on December 24, 1814, with the signing of the Treaty of Ghent.

Ripley's Aquarium of Canada

9 Ripley's Aquarium of Canada

This state-of-the-art aquarium at the base of the CN Tower features over 16,000 marine animals in 50 exhibits, with a capacity of 5.7 million liters of water. The Dangerous Lagoon features three different types of shark and has North America's longest underwater viewing tunnel at 315 ft (96 m) *(see pp22–3)*.

10 Toronto Music Garden

This playfully elegant garden, a collaboration between famed cellist Yo Yo Ma, landscape architect Julie Moir Messervy, and Toronto landscape architects, was inspired by J. S. Bach's *First Suite for Unaccompanied Cello*. Each dance movement in the suite – allemande, courante, sarabande, menuett, and gigue – plus a prelude, is represented by the plantings in one of the six sections of the garden. Summer concerts are held from July through September. ✪ *475 Queens Quay W • Map H6 • 416 973 4000 • www.harbourfront centre.com/summermusic*

Toronto Music Garden

An Art Walk

> **Morning**

🕐 Start at **Commerce Court North** *(see p66)* to admire the stunning lobby. Walk west to Bay St and the **TD Centre**, noting the **Wall and Chairs** sculpture in the plaza *(see p37)* and Joe Fafard's **bronze cows** on the lawn behind 77 King St W.

Just around the corner at 234 Bay St is the **Design Exchange** *(see p66)* then head north up Bay St to **Mercatto** *(see p69)* for an Italian lunch.

> **Afternoon**

Zigzag your way to Simcoe Park, on Front St west of Simcoe, and enjoy the luminous **Anish Kapoor sculpture**. Continue west along Front, past the CBC at No. 250, noting the **Glenn Gould sculpture**, in memory of the eccentric pianist. You'll soon come to the Rogers Centre, and **The Audience**, Michael Snow's larger-than-life fans *(see p62)*.

Turn left on Spadina Ave; crossing the bridge, look to your left to see **Eldon Garnet's memorial** commemorating Chinese laborers who helped build Canada's railroad. Continue south down Spadina turning right onto Fort York Blvd, where you'll find **Canoe Landing Park** *(see p37)*. Head back to Spadina from where it's five minutes to the lake and, just west on Queens Quay, **Toronto Music Garden**. Wander this oasis, then walk 15 minutes east to **Harbourfront Centre** *(see p63)*.

End the day with a steak dinner at **Harbour Sixty** (60 Harbour St), in the opulent former Harbour Commission building.

Left **Fairmont Royal York** Right **Steam Whistle Brewing**

🔟 Best of the Rest

1 Toronto Railway Museum
Diesel and steam engines, and rolling stock stand proud on the turntable of the John Street Roundhouse. Miniature train rides in summer. ◈ 255 Bremner Blvd • Map J5 • Open noon–5pm Wed–Sun • Adm

2 401 Richmond Street
Many of the city's best artist-run galleries are here in this gorgeous old warehouse. Find great gifts and reading material at Swipe Design – Books + Objects. ◈ 401 Richmond St W • Map H4

3 Design Exchange
This gallery showcases innovative Canadian postwar design (see p34). ◈ 234 Bay St • Map K4 • Open 10am–5pm Mon–Fri, noon–5pm Sat–Sun • Adm to special exhibits

4 Toronto Dominion Gallery of Inuit Art
An outstanding collection of postwar Inuit sculpture (see p35). ◈ 79 Wellington St W • Map K4 • Open 8am–6pm Mon–Fri, 10am–4pm Sat–Sun

5 Steam Whistle Brewing
This railroad roundhouse now functions as a microbrewery. Tour the facilities, then sample the beer. ◈ 255 Bremner Blvd • Map J5 • Open noon–6pm Mon–Thu, 11am–6pm Fri–Sun

6 Commerce Court North
The star of Toronto's early skyscrapers, this massive 34-story Romanesque structure housing the Canadian Imperial Bank of Commerce was the tallest building in Canada when completed in 1931. Today it matches aesthetically, if not in height, its towering neighbors. ◈ 25 King St W • Map L4

7 Fairmont Royal York
This grand château-style hotel (see p116), once the largest in the British Commonwealth, was built in 1928 by the Canadian Pacific Railway. ◈ 100 Front St W • Map K5

8 Air Canada Centre
Home to basketball's Raptors and hockey's Maple Leafs, the arena is in the old Toronto Postal Delivery Building. Carvings on the façade depict the history of communications. ◈ 40 Bay St • Map K5

9 Exhibition Place
Princes' Gates herald the entrance to the Canadian National Exhibition's fairgrounds, hosting major events such as the Royal Agricultural Winter Fair. ◈ Map A5

10 Power Plant Contemporary Art Gallery
Toronto's premiere contemporary art public gallery. ◈ 231 Queens Quay W • Map K6 • open 10am–5pm Tue–Sun (until 8pm Thu); holiday Mondays

Left **Wheat Sheaf Tavern** Right **Bar at Canoe**

TOP 10 Bars & Clubs

1 Crush
Wine is king at this hip loft-space bar/restaurant, but other, equally delicious, libations are also poured *(see p56)*. ⓢ *455 King St W • Map H4 • 416 977 1234 • Closed Sun in winter*

2 Bar at Canoe
It's a heady experience sipping the perfect martini while gazing at the city from the top of a skyscraper. Bar at Canoe is the place to come for after-work power drinks *(see p57)*. ⓢ *66 Wellington St W • Map K4 • 416 364 0054 • Closed weekends*

3 The Fifth Social Club
Savor the bouncer escort to the fifth-floor bar, or pass muster to enter the two-level club and dance the night away to R&B and top 40 hits *(see p57)*. ⓢ *225 Richmond St W (enter via alley) • Map J4 • 416 979 3000 • open Thu–Sat • Adm*

4 Library Bar
Tucked inside the Fairmont Royal York hotel *(see p66)*, this bar has a gentleman's-club atmosphere, with its book-lined walls and leather chairs. The cocktails are great and afternoon tea is also served. ⓢ *100 Front St W • Map K5 • 416 860 5004*

5 Bar Hop
This place takes craft beer seriously. Choose from the 36 taps or from the seven-page beer menu. ⓢ *391 King St W • Map H4 • 647 352 7476*

6 C Lounge
The spa-inspired C Lounge's chic patio attracts a hip crowd who come to sip cocktails and lounge in the intimate cabanas around the pool. ⓢ *456 Wellington St W • Map H4 • 416 260 9393*

7 Real Sports Bar & Grill
This fanatical sports bar boasts a 49-ft (14-m) HD big screen, plus 199 smaller tv sets. ⓢ *15 York St on Maple Leaf Square • Map K5 • 416 815 7325*

8 Wheat Sheaf Tavern
Toronto's oldest tavern dates back to 1849. Enjoy chicken wings and a pint with TV sports, or go out on the deck. ⓢ *667 King St W • Map G4 • 416 504 9912*

9 Maison Mercer
This club pulls in some big name DJs. The brilliant roof terrace is open in summer. ⓢ *15 Mercer St • Map J4 • 416 341 7777*

10 Brassaii
A sophisticated place for a big night out. Great food followed by dancing on Wednesday and Saturday evening *(see p69)*. ⓢ *461 King St W • Map C5 • 416 598 4730*

Note: *Patrons of Toronto bars and clubs must be of legal drinking age – 19 years or older – unless an event is specifically all-ages*

67

Left **Princess of Wales Theatre** Right **Elgin Theatre**

⁗10 Theaters

1 Ed Mirvish Theatre
Big musicals have replaced vaudeville on the bill. The 1920s interior is a fantasy of gilt-framed mirrors and chandeliers, a magnificent staircase and dome.
◈ 244 Victoria St • Map L3 • 416 872 1212

2 Royal Alexandra Theatre
Saved from demolition, this 1906 theater has been returned to Edwardian finery. A lovely mural tops the dramatic proscenium arch. Musicals and drama. ◈ 260 King St W • Map J4 • 416 872 1212

3 Princess of Wales Theatre
This venue for hit musicals opened in 1993, the first privately developed large theater the city had seen since 1907. The interior by Toronto design team Yabu Pushelberg spares no expense. Wall and ceiling murals by American minimalist Frank Stella.
◈ 300 King St W • Map J4 • 416 872 1212

4 Fleck Dance Theatre
The crème de la crème of modern dance, by both local and visiting companies, has graced this stage. ◈ 207 Queens Quay W • Map K6 • 416 973 4000

5 Elgin Theatre
The lower half of the double-decker Elgin and Winter Garden Theatre Centre was built in 1913 as a movie house and, with its lavish gilding and pro-scenium arch, is a historic gem.
◈ 189 Yonge St • Map L3 • 1 855 622 2787 (tickets), 416 314 2871 (tours)

6 Winter Garden Theatre
This room high above Elgin Theatre is aptly named. On the ceiling, some 5,000 beech leaves glitter in the lantern light. ◈ 189 Yonge St • Map L3 • 1 855 622 2787 (tickets), 416 314 2871 (tours)

7 Theatre Passe Muraille
This two-stage venue has led the way with innovative Canadian productions since the 1960s, when it launched works developed by troupes of actors. ◈ 16 Ryerson Ave • Map G3 • 416 504 7529

8 Factory Theatre
One of Toronto's oldest houses shows works by Canadian playwrights. Many masters, including local George F. Walker, got their start here. ◈ 125 Bathurst St • Map G4 • 416 504 9971

9 Bluma Appel Theatre
Devoted fans of CanStage's contemporary drama fill the seats (see p44). ◈ 27 Front St E • Map L5 • 416 366 7723

10 Young People's Theatre
This award-winning theatre produces innovative plays for the young (see p49).

Tours of the Elgin and Winter Garden theaters (5pm Thu & 11am Sat, $12) include a peek at a vaudeville-era dressing room

Around Town – Harbourfront & the Financial District

Above **Rodney's Oyster House**

Restaurants

1 Canoe
Upscale Canadian dishes – think elk and wild char – are the *pièces de résistance* from chef John Horne's kitchen. Views from this 54th-floor room are stunning. Closed weekends. ✆ *66 Wellington St W • Map K4 • 416 364 0054 • $$$$$*

2 Bymark
Some of the freshest fish in town and extravagant *foie gras* attract a well-heeled crowd. Top selection of boutique Californian wines. ✆ *66 Wellington St W • Map K4 • 416 777 1144 • $$$$$*

3 Le Sélect Bistro
A lively and much-loved French restaurant. Classy curved booths and an encyclopaedic wine list. ✆ *432 Wellington St West • Map H4 • 416 596 6405 • $$$*

4 Marben
With a fine selection of both vegetarian and meat dishes, Marben's serves up delicious, creative cuisine. Impressive cocktails. ✆ *488 Wellington St W • Map C5 • 416 979 1990 • $$$*

5 Brassaii
Nestled in a romantic cobblestone courtyard is this stunningly modern restaurant in an old warehouse building. Chef Marcus Monteiro's delicious Mediterranean cuisine draws a trendy crowd for breakfast, brunch, lunch, and late dinners. ✆ *461 King St W • Map C5 • 416 598 4730 • $$$*

6 Mercatto
Find home-cooked food and excellent wines at this down-to-earth eatery. Popular with locals on weekdays. Dinner only Sat; closed Sun. ✆ *330 Bay St • Map K4 • 416 306 0467 • $$$*

7 Rodney's Oyster House
Two dozen types of oysters entice mollusk fans; grilled fish round out the menu. ✆ *469 King St W • Map H4 • 416 363 8105 • $$$*

8 Luckee
Toronto's own superstar chef Susur Lee applies his artistry to the ultimate little-plate meal – dim sum. ✆ *328 Wellington St W • Map J4 • 416 935 0400 • $$$*

9 Jacob & Co
Dry-aged steaks cooked to perfection at this modern take on the classic steak house. A place for power lunches, but still welcoming. ✆ *12 Brant St • Map H4 • 416 366 0200 • $$$$$*

10 Jules Bistro
Authentic French bistro fare served with flair (and great *frites*). Excellent value. ✆ *147 Spadina Ave • Map H4 • 416 348 8886 • $$*

Following pages **Swan boats, Toronto Islands**

Left **City Hall** Right **Kensington Market**

Downtown

TORONTO IS A CITY OF NEIGHBORHOODS, each with a distinct identity, many with an ethnic flavor, making it the most multicultural of North American cities. In Chinatown, wares from energetic vendors compete with shoppers for sidewalk space, and restaurants offer everything from take-out buns to sit-down banquets. The city's multicultural mix finds its fullest expression in Kensington Market, where Jamaican patty shops rub shoulders with Portuguese fish vendors and Latin American empanada stalls. Farther west is the Italian enclave of Little Italy, centered along College Street. Along with this heady ethnic mix, the downtown core is home to the upscale shopping area Yorkville and many fine cultural institutions, such as the Royal Ontario Museum and the Art Gallery of Ontario.

Stone gargoyle, Casa Loma

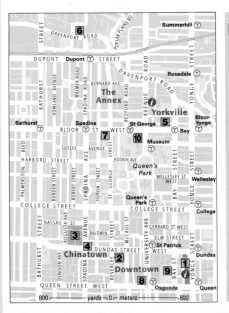

🔟 Sights

1. Toronto Eaton Centre
2. Art Gallery of Ontario
3. Kensington Market
4. Chinatown
5. Yorkville
6. Casa Loma
7. Bata Shoe Museum
8. Campbell House
9. City Hall
10. Royal Ontario Museum

Atrium, Toronto Eaton Centre

Toronto Eaton Centre
While it might seem strange that a shopping center is among the city's most popular tourist attractions – according to the numbers, at any rate – this retail complex is simply a popular place to shop, meet, hang out, and people-watch. (Crowds of boisterous teenagers attest to this fact.) Its massive size – more than 300 stores – ensures that you can find practically anything you would want to buy here. Numerous restaurants, fast-food counters, and specialty treat shops round out the choices *(see pp24–5)*.

Art Gallery of Ontario
Particularly strong in historical and contemporary Canadian works, and host to important exhibitions, this is one of the country's top art galleries *(see pp16–17)*.

Kensington Market
This funky neighborhood, in a small pocket west of Spadina, is the heart of multicultural Toronto – a place where vendors from almost every corner of the globe have set up shop. Spilling out into the narrow sidewalks are stores selling an array of fruits, vegetables, and bulk dry goods, while music blasts from open doors and loudspeakers. Pedestrians jostle with cyclists and traffic moves at a snail's pace, everyone vying for their inch of street space, particularly on Saturdays when the area is at its liveliest best. Leave the car behind and wander through the streets, soaking up the atmosphere, perhaps checking out the price of live lobster at a fish vendor's or browsing through trinkets and secondhand clothes in the many eclectic stores at the south end of Kensington Avenue *(see p58).* ⦿ *Map H2*

Chinatown
A steady flow of new Chinese immigrants keeps Toronto's main Chinatown one of the most vibrant in North America. Hundreds of authentic restaurants cater to all tastes and budgets, and there are countless shops selling Oriental wares. Spadina Avenue has also expanded to include many Vietnamese shops and restaurants *(see p38).* ⦿ *Map H2–H3*

Chinatown

Yorkville

5 Yorkville

In the 1960s, it was ground zero for hippies and the youth culture; today, this neighborhood is ground zero for establishment culture and the city's most upscale shopping. Expensive shops on Cumberland St and Yorkville Ave, between Bay St and Avenue Rd, sell luxury goods such as cosmetics, jewelry, designer fashions, antiques, and leather luggage. The area's numerous restaurants and bars cater to equally refined palates and wallets. There are also numerous fine-art galleries in the area, exhibiting some of the country's top names. Sidewalk cafés provide stylish perches for people-watching (see p38). ◈ Map C3–D3

6 Casa Loma

Styled like a medieval castle, this grand mansion is a monument to the singular tastes and vision of Sir Henry Pellatt, a prominent financier who in 1911 commissioned renowned architect E. J. Lennox to build him a home. This immense architectural undertaking was on a scale never before seen in a private Canadian residence, with plans for 98 rooms, 12 baths, 5,000 electric lights, and an elevator. Its $3.5 million cost helped bankrupt Sir Henry less than 10 years after he and his wife moved in, but its opulence remains evident in the extravagant, restored rooms and furnishings (see pp18–19).

7 Bata Shoe Museum

This unusual, specialized museum celebrates footwear form and function throughout the ages and around the world. The building's playful design, echoing a stylized shoebox, houses four galleries exhibiting everything from Roman sandals to Elton John's platform boots, as well as a history of socks and other hosiery. The exhibit of Chinese bound-foot shoes is not for the squeamish. Founded by Sonia Bata, who has scoured the world for shoes of every description, the museum also holds interesting themed exhibitions (see p35). ◈ 327 Bloor St W • Map C3 • Open 10am–5pm Mon–Sat, noon–5pm Sun • Adm

Bata Shoe Museum

Natural Air Conditioning

During the hot and humid days of a Toronto summer, Lake Ontario water does double duty. An innovative project utilizes the cold temperature of deep lake water – from intake pipes 3 miles (5 km) out from shore, and 270 ft (83 m) deep – to provide chilled energy for air conditioning Toronto's downtown high-rises and large facilities such as the Air Canada Centre (see p66). After the transfer of energy, the water is returned not to the lake but to the city's water supply system, where it serves another crucial cooling function – as drinking water.

Campbell House

Campbell House

8 The oldest remaining building from the town of York, which in 1834 became Toronto, this Georgian mansion was built in 1822 for William Campbell, an Upper Canada judge. In 1972, the 300-ton building was moved from its original location on Adelaide St to its present location, restored, and opened to the public. Guided tours are available.
⊙ *160 Queen St W • Map K3 • 416 597 0227 • Open 9:30am–4:30pm Tue–Fri, noon–4:30pm Sat & Sun (Sundays only Jun–Aug); closed Jan, Good Fri–Easter Mon, Thanksgiving weekend, Dec 25–31 • Adm*

City Hall

9 When first opened in 1965, the result of an international design competition won by Finnish architect Viljo Revell, this building was highly controversial. The two curving towers caused an uproar and possibly even led to the then mayor losing an election. The building has since become a prized landmark of the city, and the central plaza, Nathan Phillips Square, an animated symbol of civic life – a place for political demonstrations, winter ice skating, a summer farmers' market, outdoor concerts, and celebrations. Inside are murals and other fabulous artworks *(see p36)*.

Royal Ontario Museum

10 Canada's premiere museum has more than six million artifacts showcasing art, archeology, science, and nature *(see pp8–11)*.

A Downtown Walk

Morning

🕙 Start the day at the **Gardiner Museum of Ceramic Art** *(see p76)*, taking 90 minutes to peruse the permanent collections and visiting exhibits. On your way out, pop into the gift shop to have a look at the unique crafts.

Head north to Bloor St and turn left, walking a half block to the iron gates of **Philosophers' Walk**, beside the ROM *(see pp8–11)*. Take this charming footpath, which follows the course of the now buried Taddle Creek, exiting at Hoskin St in the heart of the University of Toronto campus *(see p76)*. Wander south to the Late Gothic Revival **Hart House**, lunching at **Gallery Grill** *(see p54)* on food that matches the impressive surroundings.

Afternoon

After lunch, poke into the stately common rooms and library of Hart House, noting the paintings throughout. Check out Canadian art at **Justina M. Barnicke Gallery**, too.

From Hart House turn right toward **University College** and some of the most historic buildings on campus. Stop by the **Laidlaw Wing** to visit the **University of Toronto Art Centre** *(see p35)*. Just to the south, on King's College Circle, is the 1906 **Convocation Hall**, with its Ionic-column-supported dome. Peek inside if the doors are unlocked.

From here, it's a couple of blocks' stroll south and west to Chinatown. Indulge in a feast at **Lee Garden** on Spadina Ave *(see p81)*.

You can take a self-guided tour of City Hall between 8:30am and 4:30pm, Mon–Fri; pick up a brochure at the info counter in the lobby

75

Left **Bloor Street** Right **Graduate House, University of Toronto**

Best of the Rest

1 Gardiner Museum of Ceramic Art
Historic and modern pieces from around the world *(see p34)*. 🔊 *111 Queen's Park • Map C3 • 416 586 8080 • Open 10am–6pm Mon–Thu, 10am–9pm Fri, 10am–5pm Sat & Sun • Adm*

2 West Queen West
A neighborhood of eclectic shops, cutting-edge galleries, and funky cafés *(see p78)*. 🔊 *Map A4–B4*

3 Bloor Street
An upscale shopping strip of high-end fashion and home-decor stores *(see p59)*. 🔊 *Map C3–D3*

4 Little Italy
Bars and restaurants buzz at night; shops and delis bustle during the day *(see p38)*. 🔊 *Map B3–B4*

5 Spadina Museum
A restored 1866 house with exhibits from the 1920s–1940s. Tours are mandatory. 🔊 *285 Spadina Rd • Map C2 • Open Jan–mid-Apr: noon–5pm Sat–Sun; mid-Apr–Aug: noon–5pm Tue–Sun; Sep–Dec: noon–4pm Tue–Fri (to 5pm Sat–Sun) • Adm*

6 Osgoode Hall
Ontario's first law school now houses upper provincial courts. The interior of this heritage building is magnificent. 🔊 *130 Queen St W • Map K3 • 416 947 3300 • Open Aug–late Jun: 11.45am–2pm Mon–Fri*

7 Old City Hall
Carved into the entranceway columns are caricatures of local politicians – with one exception – a straight-faced depiction of the architect. The building now serves as a courthouse *(see p36)*. 🔊 *60 Queen St W • Map K3*

8 The Annex
Leafy residential sidestreets and lively cafés, ethnic restaurants, pubs, and shops along Bloor Street make for a great stroll *(see p39)*. 🔊 *Map C2–C3*

9 University of Toronto
A sprawling campus of greenspaces and historic stone buildings dominates a huge swath of the central city, fanning out north, east, and west from Queen's Park up to Bloor Street. The post-modern Graduate House was a controversial addition. *(See p36.)* 🔊 *Map H1–J1*

10 Ontario Legislative Building
This stately building is set in a park dotted with statues and cannons. Visitors can watch politicians in action from the gallery or join in a tour of the building. 🔊 *1 Queen's Park • Map K1 • Open mid-May–Aug: 8:30am–5:30pm daily; Sep–mid-May: 8:30am–4:30pm Mon–Fri (tours hourly from 8:30am to 4:30pm)*

Left **Holt Renfrew** Right **Harry Rosen**

TOP10 Shopping Bloor St & Yorkville

1 William Ashley China
Fine crystal, tableware, and china, exquisite gifts, and expert staff ensure that you won't leave without some choice purchase wrapped in elegant gold paper. ✆ 55 Bloor St W • Map D3

2 Holt Renfrew
World-class department store featuring high fashion, as well as more affordable clothing from its own label, top perfumes and cosmetics, a hair salon, epicure store, café, and free personal shopping service. ✆ 50 Bloor St W • Map D3

3 George C
This store occupies a converted Victorian residence and stocks exclusive and adventurous high fashion for men and women. The selectively curated and reverently displayed pieces include exquisitely crafted boots by Rocco P and leather fashions by Drome. ✆ 21 Hazleton Ave • Map C2

4 Harry Rosen
Head-to-toe service is writ large at this menswear store featuring apparel from top design houses, Canali and Hugo Boss included. Suits, trousers, blazers, shirts, and all accessories, including shoes. ✆ 82 Bloor St W • Map C3

5 David's
Shoe lovers go on wild spending sprees here among the stylish footwear from hot designers. ✆ 66 Bloor St W • Map D3

6 Pusateri's
Food afficionados will love the luxury grocery items such as stuffed quail, *foie gras*, caviar, and truffle oil, and delicious prepared foods. ✆ 57 Yorkville Ave • Map D3

7 The Guild Shop
Jewelry, hand-blown glass, Inuit carvings, and more reflect the excellence of Ontario crafts. ✆ 118 Cumberland St • Map C3

8 L'Atelier Grigorian
The city's premier location for jazz, Classical, and world music. L'Atelier Grigorian has been a regular stop for audiophiles passing through the city since 1980. ✆ 70 Yorkville Ave • Map D3

9 Thomas Hinds Tobacconists
This smoker's paradise has a walk-in humidor with a full range of Cuban and Latin American cigars, and two lounges in which to enjoy them. Stellar selection of tobaccos, cigarettes, and accessories. ✆ 8 Cumberland St • Map D3

10 Roots
Quality sportswear, casual clothes, and leather goods for every member of the family. ✆ 80 Bloor St W • Map C3

Left **Cabaret** Right **Lady Mosquito**

🔟 West Queen West Shops

1 Morba
Mid-century modern emporium with loads of second-hand teak, light fixtures, and Finnish glass. Plus 1950s inspired bits-and-bobs for the kitchen and office. ◈ 665 Queen W (just west of Bathurst) • Map B4

2 C Squared
The impressive selection of Campers, Marc, and hand-crafted Cydwoqs attracts those looking for funky footwear. ◈ 693 Queen St W (west of Bathurst) • Map B4

3 Cabaret
The glamor of the 1940s and 1950s comes alive in the ball gowns, prom dresses, and costume jewelry at this Queen West mainstay. Suits and accessories for men too. Don't miss the treasures hidden in the basement. ◈ 672 Queen W (west of Palmerston Ave) • Map B4

4 Fresh Collective
This ladies' fashion shop focuses on Toronto designers. Check out Yasmine Louis's tanks and tees screen-printed with Toronto objects and journal musings. ◈ 692 Queen St W (near Euclid Ave) • Map B4

5 Coal Miner's Daughter
Pretty, alternative designs and a handmade ethos at this independent Canadian gal's boutique. Local and Swedish jewelry and vintage shoes. ◈ 744 Queen St W (at Niagara St) • Map B4

6 Type Books
A cozy independent with a great range of fiction and design titles. Inspired children's section at the back. ◈ 883 Queen St W (across from Trinity Bellwoods Park) • Map B4

7 The Paper Place
This Japanese-inspired store stocks a gorgeous selection of Chiyogami silk-screened paper. Ribbon, cards, and wrapping paper too. ◈ 887 Queen St W • Map B4

8 Fred Perry
Mod-style from this UK designer chain with Laurel-insignia collared tees, natty trainers, and classic leather sports bags. ◈ 964 Queen W • Map A4

9 Lady Mosquito
The bright, handmade accessories here include jewelry, bags, purses, and embroidered belts, all by South American artisans. ◈ 1020 Queen St W (west of Ossington) • Map A4

10 Drake General Store
Attached to The Drake's Hotel, this Canadiana shop is a great place to shop for gifts. Branches at Yonge and Eglinton and in the Bay at Yonge and Queen. ◈ 1144 Queen W (at Beaconsfield Ave) • Map A4

To keep on shopping, head north on Ossington for independents, designer, and vintages stores

Price Categories

Price categories include a three-course meal for one, half a bottle of wine, and all unavoidable extra charges including tax.	**$** under $30
	$$ $30–$50
	$$$ $50–$80
	$$$$ $80–$110
	$$$$$ over $110

Above **Opus**

🔟 Restaurants & Cafés

1 Loire
Frogs' legs and charcuterie star alongside classic Gallic fare such as *bavette* steak and duck leg confit at this modern, unpretentious bistro. ◎ *119 Harbord St • Map C3 • 416 850 8330 • $$$*

2 Fresh
A vegetarian eatery providing a filling meal and loads of choice. Noodle bowls and vitamin-packed juices suit all who need a healthy pick-up. Branches at Queen W and Crawford, and Richmond and Spadina. ◎ *326 Bloor St W • Map C4 • 416 599 4442 • $*

3 Opus
This refined dining room has one of the best wine lists in the city. Tuna tartare with caviar, and the roasted meats get top marks. ◎ *37 Prince Arthur Ave • Map C3 • 416 921 3105 • $$$$*

4 Terroni
Shabby chic Italian trattoria serving an extensive menu of regional, rustic fare. Branches at Adelaide E and Victoria, and Yonge south of Summerhill. ◎ *720 Queen St W • Map B4 • 416 504 0320 • $$*

5 Czehoski
This Queen West eatery offers one of the freshest menus in the city, with unique and sometimes eccentric flavor pairings. Popular with the professional, early-30s crowd. Open from 4pm. ◎ *678 Queen St W • Map B4 • 416 366 6111 • $$$*

6 Queen Mother Café
Thai and Laotian flavors characterize the menu at this established spot; pictures of the Queen Mum provide the decor. Opt for a cozy booth, or ask for the secluded back patio. Wicked desserts. ◎ *208 Queen St W • Map K3 • 416 598 4719 • $*

7 Nota Bene
With a lively cocktail scene and a dining room that's been called Canada's best, this is the perfect spot for a pre-theater dinner or late-night rendezvous with a cheese plate. ◎ *180 Queen St W • Map C5 • 416 977 6400 • $$$$$*

8 7 West Café
Warm and cozy, thanks to a fireplace and numerous rooms, though it can get crowded. Salads, sandwiches, pastas, and desserts are dished up 24/7. ◎ *7 Charles St W • Map D3 • 416 928 9041 • $*

9 Dark Horse Espresso Bar
For the best espresso in town, it has to be the Dark Horse: its personal feel and great quality coffee make it the ideal spot for a pick-me-up. ◎ *215 Spadina Ave • Map H3 • 416 979 1200 • $*

10 La Palette
This bohemian space tempts with good-value French food, and takes its pedigree to heart, offering horse tenderloin to adventurous diners. Fine wines and local craft beers. ◎ *492 Queen St W • Map H2 • 416 929 4900 • $$$*

Left **Bedford Academy** Right **The Roof Lounge**

Bars & Pubs

The Queen and Beaver
1 This quirky take on an English pub puts an equally tasty twist on its fare – try the unusual stilton ice cream. ◉ 35 Elm St • Map L2 • 647 347 2712

Dog and Bear
2 A cavernous friendly pub hung with Union Jacks and sporting dark red flocked wall paper. Sports-mad with numerous screens, but DJs add a lively scene on weekend evenings. ◉ 1100 Queen St W • Map A4 • 647 352 8601

dBar
3 Unwind at the end of a day's sightseeing as you linger over a cocktail or glass of crisp chardonnay in this chic bar. High people-watching factor (see p56). ◉ 60 Yorkville Ave • Map D3 • 416 963 6010

The Roof Lounge
4 Snag a seat on the 18th-floor terrace for the view, or savor the warm atmosphere inside while watching a master bartender at work (see p56). ◉ 4 Avenue Rd • Map C2 • 416 924 5471

Lula Lounge
5 Sexy salsa gets your hips swaying as rum cocktails loosen you up at this Little Portugal hotspot (see p57). ◉ 1585 Dundas St W • Map A4 • 416 588 0307 • Adm

Cameron House
6 Hang out with the locals and catch great local roots, folk, and indie bands in this ornate yet very casual bar. The changing murals on the facade are a Queen St landmark (see p56). ◉ 408 Queen St W • Map H3 • 416 703 0811 • Adm to backroom shows

180 Panorama
7 Not for acrophobics, this bar's patios, on the 51st floor of the ManuLife Centre, are the city's highest, offering spectacular views. Extensive cocktail list. ◉ 55 Bloor St W • Map D3 • 416 967 0000 • Adm

Bedford Academy
8 With 16 beers on tap, reasonably priced cocktails, TVs to catch the sports game, and a lovely patio in summer, it's no wonder this place is popular with students from nearby University of Toronto (see p76). ◉ 36 Prince Arthur Ave • Map C3 • 416 921 4600

The Paddock
9 Although red leather banquettes prompt a twinge of 1950s nostalgia, this bar is firmly rooted in the 21st century with an inventive cocktail menu and good selection of draft beers. ◉ 178 Bathurst St • Map G4 • 416 504 9997

The Drake Lounge
10 Recline on a comfy sofa beside the fireplace while taking in the scene, including the Raw Bar peddling its oysters. Then check out the live music or art happening downstairs in the Underground. ◉ 1150 Queen St W • Map A4 • 416 531 5042

Price Categories

Price categories include a three-course meal for one, half a bottle of wine, and all unavoidable extra charges including tax.

$	under $30
$$	$30–$50
$$$	$50–$80
$$$$	$80–$110
$$$$$	over $110

Above *Sashimi* and *maki*, Sashimi Island

🔟 Ethnic Eats

1 Bahn Mi Boys
Traditional Vietnamese *bahn mi* baguettes (stuffed with grilled pork, sausage or paté, grated veg and cilantro) are served with pulled pork or squid. Try the kimchi fries. Branches at Queen/Spadina and Yonge/Gerrard. ◈ *399 Yonge St • Map L2 • 416 977 0303 • $*

2 93 Harbord
Meze are updated in this Middle Eastern standout, with addictive *hummus* and *musakhan* – a mix of chicken, onions, and pine nuts, and mains that include lamb tagine in a fig and shiraz sauce: divine! ◈ *93 Harbord St • Map B3 • 416 922 5914 • $$*

3 Boulevard Café
The city's oldest Peruvian restaurant offers grilled meats and excellent seafood specialties. Tapas and drinks served in the upstairs lounge; lovely patio in summer. ◈ *161 Harbord St • Map C3 • 416 961 7676 • $$$*

4 Lee Garden
This Cantonese restaurant is the place to go for tasty chow mein, barbecued pork, and fresh seafood dishes. ◈ *331 Spadina Ave • Map H2 • 416 593 9524 • $$*

5 Banjara Indian Cuisine
Its unfussy, diner-like interior belies the fine Indian cooking that Banjara has become famous for. Flavors include hints of tart lemon and freshly roasted cumin. ◈ *796 Bloor St W • Map B3 • 416 963 9360 • $*

6 Korea House
This family-run restaurant cooks up traditional Korean fare, with starters such as *kimchi* (hot, pickled cabbage) and fish and meat mains. Try the unusual Korean rice wines or *soju*, strong distilled liquors flavored with fruit or flowers. ◈ *666 Bloor St W • Map B3 • 416 536 8666 • $$*

7 El Trompo
Fun, lively Mexican place right in the heart of Kensington Market. If you're lucky you'll snag a seat on the patio to take in the streetlife. ◈ *277 Augusta Ave • Map H2 • 416 260 0097 • $*

8 Sashimi Island
One of many all-you-can-eat sushi joints. Refined Japanese dining is not but if you are just after *maki* rolls, then this could well be the spot for you. ◈ *635 College St • Map B3 • 416 535 1888 • $*

9 Café Diplomatico
The patio is the place to be at this Little Italy institution *(see p38)*. Panzerotti, pizza, and pasta are on the menu, but it's the people-watching opportunities that draw the crowds. ◈ *594 College St • Map B3 • 416 534 4637 • $*

10 Julie's Cuban
Checkered table cloths, vintage salt and pepper shakers, a warm welcome, and delicious, earthy Cuban food. It's a hidden treasure. ◈ *202 Dovercourt Rd • Map A4 • 416 532 7397 • $$*

 Note: All restaurants accept credit cards and serve vegetarian meals unless otherwise stated

Left **Vegetables at St. Lawrence Market** Right **Sidewalk café, The Danforth**

East

THE EASTERN PART OF TORONTO *is a region of contrasts. Some of the city's grandest old mansions remain along the stately streets of Jarvis and Sherbourne, though many of these homes were abandoned for years and have only in the past few decades undergone renovation and gentrification. The same is true of Cabbagetown, originally a working-class Irish immigrant neighborhood, where Victorian rowhouses and cottages have been trans- formed into an upscale neighborhood of urban professionals. There are many historic sights in the area and a vibrant streetlife throughout Toronto's east side, thanks to the lively gay village along Church Street, the Greek and Macedonian enclave of The Danforth, and the fresh-food destination of St. Lawrence Market. To the south, a complex of Victorian buildings has been converted into the Distillery Historic District, one of the city's newest shopping and entertainment destinations.*

Church Street

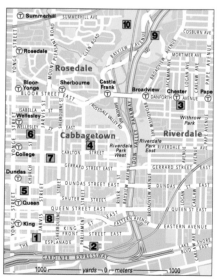

Sights

1. St. Lawrence Market
2. Distillery Historic District
3. The Danforth
4. Cabbagetown
5. Mackenzie House
6. Church Street
7. Allan Gardens
8. Toronto's First Post Office
9. Todmorden Mills Heritage Site
10. Evergreen Brick Works

Cabbagetown cottage

St. Lawrence Market
Farmers sell fresh produce and baked goods from seasonal stalls in the north market on Saturdays, with many specializing in organic food. In the vibrant south market, open Tuesday to Saturday, over 120 permanent vendors sell everything from fresh bread and produce to seafood, meats, and cheeses *(see p85)*. The south building served as City Hall in the mid- to late 1800s. ✆ *Map M5*

Distillery Historic District
This Victorian industrial district is now one of the city's most interesting and picturesque. Pedestrian-only cobblestone streets lead past old warehouses and historic factories stunningly preserved and renovated to house galleries, restaurants, performance venues, and specialty shops *(see pp20–21)*.

The Danforth
Linked to downtown by the 1918 Prince Edward Viaduct, which spans the Don River Valley, The Danforth has been called home by the city's thriving Greek and Macedonian communities since the 1950s. In early August, the weeklong Taste of The Danforth street festival is a smorgasbord of tasty treats and live entertainment *(see p39)*. ✆ *Map F3*

Cabbagetown
One of Toronto's earliest subdivisions, dating to the 1840s, this district remained a working-class community well into the 1970s. Many of the cottages and Victorian homes have since been renovated, and it is now an upscale residential enclave that makes for a pleasant stroll *(see p38)*. On the east side is Riverdale Park and its delightful Riverdale Farm *(see p48)*. Across the street, on the grounds of the Necropolis Cemetery, is a chapel built in 1872, a Gothic Revival treasure. At the north end of Cabbagetown, St. James Cemetery, Toronto's oldest, has many beautiful crypts. ✆ *Map E3–E4*

Mackenzie House
This Greek Revival rowhouse, built in 1858, was the home of Toronto's first mayor, William Lyon Mackenzie, who returned here after being granted amnesty for his leading role in the failed Upper Canada Rebellion in 1837. Now a period museum, it features a recreated printshop and a gallery with changing exhibitions. It is rumored to be haunted. ✆ *82 Bond St • Map L3 • 416 392 6915 • open Jan–Apr: noon–5pm Sat–Sun; May–early Sep: noon–5pm Tue–Sun; Sep–Dec: noon–4pm Tue–Fri, noon–5pm Sat–Sun • Adm*

Mackenzie House

The construction of the Prince Edward Viaduct is featured in Michael Ondaatje's 1987 bestselling novel **In the Skin of a Lion**

83

6 Church Street

The hub of Toronto's Gay and Lesbian Village, Church Street from Carleton Street to north of Wellesley Street, is vibrant day and night. Bars and restaurants cater to an out crowd, and specialty shops, such as those selling body wear, abound. The general vibe is pink and proud and it's no wonder that the popular TV show *Queer as Folk*, made in Toronto, is often filmed on location at Church Street. Pick up a copy of the free bi-weekly newspaper *Xtra!*, available at most shops on the street, for listings of everything the village has to offer.
⬡ *Map L1–L2*

Conservatory, Allan Gardens

Don River

Named by the lieutenant-governor of Upper Canada, John Graves Simcoe, after a stream in Yorkshire, England, the Don River is one of the city's defining natural features. Flowing just east of downtown into Lake Ontario, the river and its steep valley cut a swath through the city. While industrial use of the river, particularly at its southern end – where its meandering course is channeled into an abrupt right turn – have degraded the water, naturalization projects have started the long process of restoring the Don Valley to ecological health. The ribbon of connected greenspaces following the Don's course means that you can hike and cycle along bike paths for hours right in the center of the city and encounter few signs of civilization.

7 Allan Gardens

This large park embodies the contradictions of the downtown-eastside: It is both grand and gritty. Best explored during the day, the gardens, which first opened in 1860, contain a delightful glass-and-metal conservatory complex consisting of six greenhouses, each with a different climate zone, built in 1910. Inside, the exuberant displays of seasonal and permanent greenery and flowers delight the senses. ⬡ *Map M2*

8 Toronto's First Post Office

This working post office and museum opened in 1833 and is the only surviving example of a British-era post office in Canada. Here, you can write a letter with a quill pen and have it stamped with a distinctive cancellation mark: "York-Toronto 1833." There is also a topographic model of 1830s Toronto, period furniture, and 19th-century reproduction ink wells and sealing wax. The library, housing an extensive archival collection of postal-related materials, is open by appointment only while the museum is open for self-guided tours. ⬡ *260 Adelaide St E • Map M4 • 416 865 1833 • Open 9am–5:30pm Mon–Fri, 10am–4pm Sat, noon–4pm Sun • Adm by donation*

Toronto's First Post Office

Todmorden Mills

9 Todmorden Mills Heritage Site

This collection of late 18th-century buildings imparts the feel of a historic village. Fine examples of the original industrial architecture pepper the site. Two houses – the 1797 Terry Cottage and 1800s Helliwell House – have been restored with period furnishings. The Paper Mill Gallery and Theatre stages performances and art shows. A wildflower preserve bursts with trilliums in spring, and trails offer lots of wildlife spotting opportunities. ⊗ *67 Pottery Rd • Map F2 • Historic Buildings: open Jan–May & Sep–Dec: noon–4pm Wed–Fri (to 4:30pm Sat–Sun); Jun–Aug: 10am–4:30pm Tue–Fri (to 7:30pm Thu), noon–5pm Sat–Sun • Adm • Grounds: open daily*

10 Evergreen Brick Works

The smokestack is just one of the historic features that remain at this once-thriving industrial complex, which opened in 1889 to manufacture bricks for local buildings using clay found on site. The quarry has been returned to nature as a park with ponds and meadows, and the industrial buildings redeveloped as a sustainable development showcase. Also here is a restaurant, garden center, and adventure playground *(see p40).* ⊗ *550 Bayview Ave • Map E2*

A Cabbagetown Stroll

Morning

🕐 Begin your day with an espresso at **Jet Fuel**, 519 Parliament St. After your caffeine jolt, turn right and walk north to **Wellesley St**, then turn right again and walking east to take in the charming Victorian architecture. Note the strange animal and face carvings on **No. 314**. Explore the lanes running northward, including **Wellesley Cottages**, a courtyard tucked behind the street with seven gabled cottages. As you come to the end of Wellesley St, spend a few moments wandering through **Wellesley Park**, enjoying the view across the Don Valley.

Backtrack to Wellesley St and turn left onto **Sumach St**, its charming houses classic Cabbagetown. Note Second Empire-style **No. 420–422**, built in 1886, and the English cottage style of **Nos. 404–408**. Turn left at Winchester St; **Necropolis Cemetery**, Toronto's oldest non-denominational graveyard, will be on the left. Peek into the **chapel** to admire the stained-glass windows.

Afternoon

For lunch, head back along Winchester St to Parliament St, turning left to Carlton St, where you'll find **Japanese Omi**.

After lunch, continue to meander the area's compact streets – Metcalfe, Salisbury, and Sackville – before walking east to **Riverdale Park** and its **Riverdale Farm** *(see p48).* Across the street from the park's northwest corner is cute **Winchester Café**, dispensing refreshments through a side window.

294

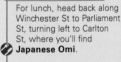

296

Left **South Market** Right **Outdoor vendors, North Market**

TOP 10 St. Lawrence Market

1 South Market
Opened in 1844 as Toronto's second City Hall, this building had a police station on the first floor and a jail in the basement. Today it houses a thriving public market – and some of the tastiest, freshest meats, cheese, produce, and breads around.
91 Front St E • Open 8am–6pm Tue–Thu, 8am–7pm Fri, 5am–5pm Sat

2 North Market
Buy fruits, vegetables, and herbs directly from those who grow them. Organic items and home-baked treats, too. *92 Front St E • Open 5am–early afternoon Sat*

3 Outdoor Stands
Sprawling on the sidewalks outside the North Market, these produce and flower stalls only add to the boisterous atmosphere of market Saturdays. For the best selection, arrive early in the morning.

4 Antique Market
From 5am every Sunday, vendors pack the North Market with piles of knick-knacks as well as more serious pieces including military collectibles and mid-century design classics.

5 Montreal Bagels
Locals love St. Urbain Bakery's dense, chewy buns, in the South Market. The bagel-cooking method – boil then bake in a wood-fired oven – hails from French-Canadian city Montreal.

6 Alex Farms
A cheese lover's paradise, in South Market, selling every kind of cheese imaginable, from French cantal to the most pungent of blues. Good raw-milk cheese selection.

7 Buskers and Craft-Sellers
Lively street action is part of the charm of market Saturdays, as buskers entertain and craftspeople ply their wares outside both the north and south buildings.

8 Peameal Bacon Sandwiches
Quintessentially Canadian, and perfect to fuel up for the day, the kaiser buns at South Market's Carousel Bakery are stuffed with salty, peameal-encrusted pork.

9 Market Gallery
Artifacts and photographs of Toronto's history are exhibited in free, themed shows, in the old council chamber tucked on the second floor of the South Market. See the market from a different perspective, through the large window looking out onto the floor. *Open 10am–4pm Tue–Fri, 9am–4pm Sat*

10 South Market – Lower Floor
Below the market's main floor are smaller stalls with items such as accessories and hats, and jams and chutneys. There are a couple of health-food stores, some green grocers, and a tea shop.

Several pay-parking lots are near the market; the two closest are on Jarvis St south of Front, and on Market St south of the Esplanade

Left **Lileo** Right **Ethel**

🔟 Shopping East

John Fluevog
Bad-boy cobbler Fluevog, who hails from Vancouver and has been making his solid, unusual shoes for years, now sells his footwear in the vibrant Distillery District's Boiler House Complex. 🗊 *4 Trinity St • Map E5 • 416 583 1970*

Negash & Dessa
For the professional woman, there's everything one could want here: a sophisticated range of leather goods, and sleek silver jewelry too. 🗊 *161 Danforth Ave • Map F3 • 416 462 9306*

The Big Carrot
Lovers of organic foods and natural body care will love this large and well-stocked grocery store. Recharge with a sampling of the delicious prepared foods and organic juices on offer here. 🗊 *Carrot Common Complex, 348 Danforth Ave • Map F3 • 416 466 2129*

Soma Chocolate
A store for the chocolate cognoscenti. Sample the divine confections or try a cup of steaming Mayan hot chocolate, redolent with spices. 🗊 *32 Tank House Lane • Map E5 • 416 815 7662*

Lileo
A huge selection of men's and women's fashions, plus handbags, books, CDs, and limited-edition running shoes. A juice bar with a raw-food menu will keep appetites at bay. 🗊 *12 Trinity St, Bldg 35 • Map E5 • 416 413 1410*

Artsmarket
Artists, vintage collectors, and crafts people display their vastly differing wares in small, close-knit spaces. Good fun on a lively Leslieville block. 🗊 *1114 Queen St E • Map F4 • 416 546 8464*

Ethel
Elegant teak buffets and dining tables, glass and acrylic coffee tables, and other nifty pieces from the 1960s and 1970s, at reasonable prices. 🗊 *327 Queen St E • Map E4 • 416 778 6608*

Gadabout
Get lost in time at this tiny vintage store in Leslieville. Oddments from around the globe are packed into display cases and there are plenty of vintage finds to add to your wardrobe. 🗊 *1300 Queen St E • Map F4 • 416 463 1254*

Kristapsons
Pacific salmon, cold-smoked on the premises using a secret recipe, is all you'll find in this store – but what a find. Those in the know claim it ranks among the world's best. 🗊 *1095 Queen St E • Map F4 • 416 466 5152*

Henry's
Everything a photographer needs, from the latest digital cameras to vintage Leica lenses, and necessities such as film, batteries, photo paper, and a quality developing service. Knowledgeable, helpful staff. 🗊 *119 Church St • Map L4 • 416 868 0872*

Left **Dora Keogh** Right **Irish Embassy Pub and Grill**

Bars & Pubs

1 Consort Bar
Relish the great whiskeys and masterfully mixed cocktails in this dignified bar at the Omni King Edward Hotel *(see p116)*. ⓢ 37 King St E • Map L4 • 416 863 3131

2 Betty's
This popular pub offers beers on tap, tasty food such as burgers and Montreal smoked meat on rye, billiard tables, and a great patio. ⓢ 240 King St E • Map M4 • 416 368 1300

3 Mill Street Brew Pub
Sample the 13 Mill Street brews on tap while gazing on the vats of beer fermenting in the glass-walled brewery. ⓢ 21 Tank House Lane • Map E5 • 416 681 0338

4 C'est What?
A casual spot with 35 microbrews on tap, some, such as the hemp, rye, and coffee brews, produced exclusively for the pub. Live music some nights and Sunday afternoons. ⓢ 67 Front St E • Map L5 • 416 867 9499

5 Irish Embassy Pub and Grill
Savor a drink at the bar or delicious pub food featuring Irish specialities while sitting on a comfy banquette. The high ceilings and big windows keep it airy. ⓢ 49 Yonge St • Map L5 • 416 866 8282

6 Dora Keogh
A reconstructed 1890s Irish pub, with dark-wood benches, low stools and little tables. Good selection of beers and whiskeys.

Live music is on most nights. ⓢ 141 Danforth Ave • Map F3 • 416 778 1804

7 Pravda Vodka House
Enjoy Russian-inspired dishes and an endless selection of vodka at this club-like restaurant with Soviet-themed decor. ⓢ 44 Wellington St E • Map L4 • 416 366 0303

8 Imperial Pub Tavern
Regulars, students, and old-timers treasure the circular bar and jukeboxes playing old jazz hits in this no-frills place. ⓢ 54 Dundas St E • Map L3 • 416 977 4667

9 Ceílí Cottage
Snug, rustic Irish bar with excellent food, run by the champion oyster shucker from Starfish *(see p52)*. Good hand-pulled beer, no bottles. ⓢ 1301 Queen St E • Map F4 • 416 406 1301

10 BeerBistro
Beer is taken seriously here with an enormous selection to please all tastes. Many menu items incorporate beers too. ⓢ 18 King St E • Map L4 • 416 861 9872

Price Categories

Price categories include a three-course meal for one, half a bottle of wine, and all unavoidable extra charges including tax.

$	under $30
$$	$30–$50
$$$	$50–$80
$$$$	$80–$110
$$$$$	over $110

Above **Pizza Libreto**

Restaurants

1 Ruby Watchco
Chef Lynn Crawford's Home-style concept dining is popular. Menus change daily. ◈ 730 Queen St E • Map F4 • 416 465 0100 • $$$

2 Pizza Libreto
This lively spot serves up the most authentic Neapolitan pizzas in town. Reserve ahead or perch at the window. ◈ 550 Danforth Ave • Map F3 • 416 466 0400 • $$

3 Gilead Café and Wine Bar
Try local culinary legend Jamie Kennedy's creative sandwiches at lunch or impeccable mains at dinner. Seasonal menus change daily. ◈ 4 Gilead Place • Map E5 • 647 288 0680 • $$$

4 Batifole
Francophiles flock to this unpretentious restaurant for such classics as *cassoulet* and *soupe de poissons*, on the outer edge of Chinatown East. ◈ 744 Gerrard St E • Map F4 • 416 462 9965 • $$

5 Rock Lobster
This casual spot serves up luscious lobster rolls, best washed down with their infamous Bloody Caesar. ◈ 1192 Queen St E • Map B4 • 416 533 1800 • $$

6 Allen's
Grab a wooden booth at the front of this pub-cum-restaurant. Steak, salmon, and lamb, all local and pesticide free where possible. ◈ 143 Danforth Ave • Map F3 • 416 463 3086 • $$

7 Pan on the Danforth
The familiar Greek favorites are served here, but lesser-known dishes like *kakavia*, a fish stew, and home-made fig and port ice cream are standouts. ◈ 516 Danforth Ave • Map F3 • 416 466 8158 • $$

8 El Catrin
Located in the old boiler house complex in the Distillery District *(see pp20–21)*, this huge Mexican restaurant has wild Day-of-the-Dead themed decor. ◈ 18 Tank House Lane • Map E5 • 416 203 2121 • $$$

9 Hiro Sushi
Diners feast on grilled tuna, *sashimi*, *wasabi*-spiked fish, and other Japanese delights, accompanied by fine sakes. ◈ 171 King St E • Map M4 • 416 304 0550 • $$$

10 Gio Rana's Really, Really Nice Restaurant
This unconventionally named and decorated restaurant is housed in a former bank and specializes in great-value southern Italian fare. Open kitchen. ◈ 1220 Queen St E • Map B4 • 416 469 5225 • $$

Note: *All restaurants accept credit cards and serve vegetarian meals unless otherwise stated*

Left **Ashbridges Bay Park, The Beach** Right **Canada's Wonderland**

Greater Toronto

THE AREA SURROUNDING THE CITY PROPER *has expanded rapidly in the last few decades, with suburban bedroom communities popping up around the urban fringe, engulfing fertile farmland. While highway development ensures convenient access to the many sites outside the city, roads can be extremely crowded at rush hour, and it is a good idea to plan excursions for off-peak times. Many delightful parks and natural areas lie just outside the city, along with spacious beaches. Toronto Zoo, set in the huge wilderness area of Rouge National Urban Park (see p41) on the eastern edge of the city, is a delightful place to spend a day, as is, for family thrills, Canada's Wonderland. Several historic attractions, such as Black Creek Pioneer Village, where costumed guides demonstrate pioneer life, provide a glimpse into mid-19th-century country life. Art lovers are drawn due north to the renowned McMichael Canadian Art Collection in the charming village of Kleinburg.*

Polar bear, Toronto Zoo

🔟 Sights

1. McMichael Canadian Art Collection
2. Toronto Zoo
3. The Beach
4. Canada's Wonderland
5. Ontario Science Centre
6. Black Creek Pioneer Village
7. Gibson House Museum
8. Colborne Lodge
9. Legoland Discovery Centre
10. Aga Khan Museum

White Pine, McMichael Collection

1 McMichael Canadian Art Collection

Located in Kleinburg, 18 miles (30 km) from downtown Toronto, this outstanding gallery features a stellar display of works by the seminal Group of Seven painters, their contemporaries such as Tom Thomson and Emily Carr, and the artists they inspired. There's also an impressive collection of First Nations and Inuit artists. ✆ 10365 Islington Ave, Kleinburg • Map A1 • 905 893 1121 • Open May–Oct: 10am–5pm daily; Nov–Apr: 10am–4pm • Adm

2 Toronto Zoo

This 710-acre (287-ha) zoo houses some 5,000 animals representing over 500 species. Roaming freely within outdoor enclosures, large creatures such as African elephants can be seen along 6 miles (10 km) of trails. There are four tropical pavilions, each representing a distinct geographic habitat. ✆ 361A Old Finch Ave • Map B1 • 416 392 5929 • Open mid-Mar–Apr: 9:30am–4:30pm Mon–Fri, 9:30am–6pm Sat & Sun; May–Aug: 9am–7pm daily; Sep–Oct: 9:30am–4:30pm Mon–Fri, 9:30am–6pm Sat & Sun; Nov–mid-Mar: 9:30am–4:40pm daily • Adm

3 The Beach

This is one area of the city that takes full advantage of its lakeside setting, with an atmosphere that feels more like a small resort town. In summer especially, crowds throng to the white sand beaches, stroll the 2.5-mile (4-km) boardwalk, picnic in Kew Gardens, a turn-of-the-19-century park, and shop along Queen Street (see p93). The area is at its busiest in late July, during the Beaches International Jazz Festival (see p47). ✆ Map B2

4 Canada's Wonderland

This theme park north of Toronto draws crowds with over 200 attractions, 69 rides, and a huge water park. Thrills abound, the biggest pleasers being the roller coasters. ✆ 9580 Jane St, Vaughan • Map A1 • 905 832 8131 • Open mid-Jun–Aug: 10am–10pm daily; Sep: 10am–8pm Sat & Sun; Oct: 10am–5pm Sat & Sun (hours subject to change) • Adm • www.canadaswonderland.com

5 Ontario Science Centre

Exhibits in this museum are interactive and geared toward youngsters, all in the name of making science education fun. Eleven themed areas cover a diverse range of topics, including Earth's ecosystems, space, sport, communication, energy, and the human body. ✆ 770 Don Mills Rd • Map B1 • 416 696 1000 • Open 10am–4pm Mon–Fri; 10am–5pm Sat & Sun

Ontario Science Centre

6 Black Creek Pioneer Village

For an authentic taste of early settler life, visit this re-creation of a 19th-century rural Ontario community. Among the dozens of buildings – a handful original to the site, the rest moved here and restored – are a school, a church, village shops, houses, and barns. The grounds include an orchard, millpond, restored gardens, and grazing livestock. Costumed staff demonstrate pioneer crafts and carry out tasks such as tinsmithing and milling flour (the flour is available for sale). Free wagon rides are popular with the kids. ⊗ *1000 Murray Ross Pkwy • Map A1 • 416 736 1733 • Open May–Jun: 9:30am–4pm Mon–Fri, 11am–5pm Sat–Sun; Jul–Labour Day: 10am–5pm Mon–Fri, 11am–5pm Sat–Sun; Labour Day–Dec 25: 9:30am–4pm Mon–Fri, 11am–4:30pm Sat–Sun • Adm*

7 Gibson House Museum

While North York is a relentlessly modern part of the city, it is also home to this historic gem – an elegant Georgian farmhouse built in 1851. The original owner, land surveyor and mapper David Gibson, was a leader of the

Black Creek Pioneer Village

Upper Canada Rebellion in 1837 who was forced to flee to the US when the uprising failed. Following his pardon, Gibson returned and built this home for his wife and seven children. The museum hosts guided tours and also holds classes in such forgotten arts as hearth-cooking. ⊗ *5172 Yonge St • Map A1 • 416 395 7432 • Open 1–5pm Wed–Sun (Thu until 8pm); Jul & Aug from 11am • Adm*

8 Colborne Lodge

This 1837 house was the residence of land surveyor John Howard and his wife, Jemima. Howard deeded the estate to the city, thereby forming the basis for High Park *(see p40)*. Located at the south end of the park, the Regency-style house, with its gorgeous circular verandah, has been fully restored and includes many of the Howards' original belongings, including John Howard's original watercolors of early Toronto scenes. Costumed guides lead tours. Don't miss the garden, planted with kitchen herbs and flowers. Seasonal celebrations, such as the Harvest Festival and the lamplit processions at Christmastime, are very popular. ⊗ *Colborne Lodge Dr • Map A2 • 416 392 6916 • Open Jan, Feb & Apr: noon–4pm Sat & Sun; Mar: noon–4pm Thu–Sun; May–Aug: noon–5pm Tue–Sun; Sep: noon–5pm Sat & Sun; Oct–Dec: noon–4pm Tue–Sun • Adm*

R. C. Harris Filtration Plant

Built in the late 1930s, in an era when public works buildings were grand statements – expressions of engineering mastery – this filtration plant has been dubbed the "palace of purification." Monumentally perched atop a gentle hill, this Art Deco structure holds the machines that treat the city's drinking water, which is pumped into the facility from a pipe that begins 1.5 miles (3 km) offshore, in Lake Ontario. Close to 200 million gallons (757 million litres) of water are processed daily, supplying about half of Toronto's needs.

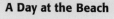

Legoland Discovery Centre

Little builders aged 3 to 10 will love this indoor complex packed with all things LEGO, including a Miniland of miniature landmarks, a LEGO car speed test track, a 4-D cinema, a soft play area, a laser ride, and millions of bricks. Adults unaccompanied by children will not be admitted.

1 Bass Pro Mills Dr, Vaughan • 1 855 356 2150 • Open 10am–7:30pm Mon–Thu, 10am–9pm Fri & Sat, 11am–7pm Sun (last admission 2 hours before closing) • Adm

Aga Khan Museum

The first museum in North America dedicated to the Arts of Islam, the Aga Khan Museum is housed in a distinctive angular building designed by Japanese architect Fumihiko Maki. Inside are Islamic treasures including ceramics, textiles, scientific texts, and musical instruments. There are also undiscovered masterpieces such as delicately painted folios from Shah-Nameh (Book of Kings), Iran, c.1522. The museum's collection highlights the cultural diversity of muslim society, from Spain, through Africa and the Middle East, to China. Two major temporary exhibitions – one contemporary, one historical – are on show, and dance and music performances run throughout the day. *77 Wynford Dr • Map B2 • Open 10am–6pm Tue–Sun (until 8pm Thu) • Adm • www.agakhanmuseum.org*

Aga Khan Museum

A Day at the Beach

Morning

Begin at **Sunset Grill**, 2006 Queen St E, for breakfast. (The waffles are a local favorite.) Fortified, cross the street and meander toward the lake through **Kew Gardens**, noting the unusual circular path and rounded windows of **Kew Williams Cottage**, built in 1902, at the park's south end. Reaching the **boardwalk**, turn right and follow it to the end, a 15 minute stroll. Look out for the paved path on the right; take it into **Ashbridges Bay Park**, where you can stroll along the waterfront, watching sailboats moor. The views across the city from the west side of the park are excellent.

For lunch, retrace your steps to Kew Gardens, then up to Queen St, for a famously good burger at **Hero Certified Burgers** (No. 2018). Eat in or take out and sit in Kew Gardens across the street.

Afternoon

Spend the afternoon browsing the shops on Queen St E, picking up a treat at **The Nutty Chocolatier**, No. 2179, to enjoy while taking a break at the serene sunken rock garden – **Ivan Forest Gardens** – at Queen St E and Glen Manor Dr.

Shopped out, snag a seat on **Outrigger's** patio (No. 2232) and relax with a refreshment. If you're up for more walking, continue another 10 minutes east to the **R. C. Harris Filtration Plant** *(see p92)* to stroll the grounds of this Art Deco gem and admire the view of the Scarborough Bluffs *(see p94)* and Lake Ontario.

Around Town – Greater Toronto

Left **Bluffer's Park** Right **Humber Arboretum**

🔟 Greenspaces

1 Rouge National Urban Park
Following the course of the Rouge River, this is one of North America's largest urban parks. It contains the wildest natural area in the city. ◈ *Map B1 • www.rouge park.com*

2 Kortright Center
This premier conservation area hosts hands-on activities and guided nature walks for all ages – the nighttime "owl prowls" are popular. Some 11 miles (18 km) of trails lead through forests, meadows, and Humber River valleylands. ◈ *9550 Pine Valley Dr, Woodbridge • Map A1 • 905 832 2289 • Adm*

3 Toronto Botanical Garden
Magnificent floral displays are to be found in this large park by the Wilket Creek ravine. Kids' activities at the superb teaching garden. ◈ *777 Lawrence Ave E • Map B1 • 416 397 1340*

4 High Park
Toronto's largest downtown park has extensive trails through woodlands and oak savanna, along with playgrounds, tennis courts, a small zoo, historic Colborne Lodge *(see p92)*, and a snack bar and restaurant. ◈ *1873 Bloor St W • Map A2*

5 Bluffer's Park
Dramatic sandstone cliffs rise 350 ft (110 m) above Lake Ontario, providing a spectacular backdrop to this east-end park. Marina and seasonal snack bar. ◈ *Brimley Rd, south end • Map B2*

6 Guildwood Park
Enjoy gardens and naturalized areas full of woodland wildflowers at this Scarborough Bluff park. Intriguing architectural artifacts saved from demolished buildings are spread throughout the grounds. ◈ *201 Guildwood Pkwy • Map B1*

7 Humber Bay Butterfly Habitat
Native flowers and shrubs attract butterflies at this lakeshore park with a great view of the city's skyline. A demonstration garden highlights butterfly-attracting flowers for home gardens. ◈ *Humber Bay Park Rd E • Map A2*

8 Sunnybrook Park
Encompassing shady Burke Ravine and two forests, this park provides respite from summer heat. Interpretive nature trails; riding stables; several sports fields; picnic tables; and restaurant. ◈ *Enter west of Leslie St via Wilket Creek Park • Map B1*

9 Martin Goodman Trail
Hugging Lake Ontario, the 12-mile (22 km) trail connects the waterfront parks and is popular with joggers, cyclists, and in-line skaters. ◈ *Map A2–B2*

10 Humber Arboretum
Set near the West Humber River, this nature center has self-guided trails through woodlands and meadows, and fine exhibits on plants and wildlife. ◈ *205 Humber College Blvd • Map A2*

Some parks close at dusk; call ahead to confirm hours. For more information on Toronto's parks, visit the website www.trca.on.ca

Price Categories

Price categories include a three-course meal for one, half a bottle of wine, and all unavoidable extra charges including tax.	**$** under $30
	$$ $30–$50
	$$$ $50–$80
	$$$$ $80–$110
	$$$$$ over $110

Above **Auberge du Pommier**

🔟 Restaurants

1 Amaya
Fresh textures and subtle spicing define the nouveau Indian cuisine at Amaya. Start off with the signature curry martini. ⬧ 1701 Bayview Ave • Map B2 • 416 322 3270 • $$

2 Scaramouche
The Pasta Bar is a Toronto institution – and less pricey than the elegant main dining room, which has been serving up inventive, consistently excellent cuisine for decades. Fabulous view of the city. ⬧ 1 Benvenuto Pl • Map C2 • 416 961 8011• $$$$$ main room; $$$ Pasta Bar

3 Grano
A cheerful, boisterous place with excellent, satisfying, Italian fare and a family atmosphere. There are lots of vegetarian options on the menu. ⬧ 2035 Yonge St • Map B2 • 416 440 1986 • $$$

4 North 44°
Chef Mark McEwan dishes up modern international cooking – French classics with sophisti-cated twists. An impressive drinks and wine list. ⬧ 2537 Yonge St • Map B1 • 416 487 4897 • $$$$$

5 Via Allegro
Authentic Italian food – pasta, seafood, and wood-fired oven pizzas – and an award-winning wine cellar which, with over 5,000 selections, is an oenophile magnet. ⬧ 1750 The Queensway • Map A2 • 416 622 6677 • $$$$

6 Sushi Kaji
Set menu options – including the deluxe, chef's choice omakase menu – present course after course of wonderful, complex Japanese creations balanced with simple, incredibly fresh, sashimi and sushi. ⬧ 860 The Queensway • Map A2 • 416 252 2166 • $$$$

7 Auberge du Pommier
Classic French cooking with a contemporary twist. Two intimate rooms, a bar, and a small patio. In winter, ask for a table by the fireplace. ⬧ 4150 Yonge St • Map B1 • 416 222 2220 • $$$$

8 Dragon Dynasty
Classic Chinese dishes more than make up for the unpromising surroundings of this restaurant, located in a mall. ⬧ 2301 Brimley Rd • Map B1 • 416 321 9000 • $$$

9 Katsura
Japanese specialties such as sushi, sashimi, tempura, and grilled fish. Diners can sit at the sushi bar, around teppan tables in the dining room, or in private tatami rooms. ⬧ Westin Prince Hotel, 900 York Mills Rd • Map B1 • 416 444 2511 • $$$$

10 Brussels Bistro
Housed in a grand Beaches residence, this authentic Belgian place serves up great mussels, bouillabaise, and bevettes. For brunch try the sinful pain perdu (French toast). ⬧ The Beach, 1975A Queen St E • 416 694 0004 • $$$

Note: All restaurants accept credit cards and serve vegetarian meals unless otherwise stated

Left **Horseshoe Falls, Niagara Falls** Right **Windmill in Goderich**

Beyond Toronto

WITHIN EASY DRIVING DISTANCE OF TORONTO are many delightful communities worthy of a daytrip or a more extended visit. North of the city, Honey Harbour and Gravenhurst are the gateways to cottage country, with beautiful lakes and forests, while Collingwood offers excellent skiing in winter and summer fun on Georgian Bay. To the west of Toronto are many charming small towns, such as Stratford, with its world-renowned Shake-spearean theater festival, and the Mennonite community of St. Jacobs. Further west, along the shores of Lake Huron, wide sandy beaches stretching north and south of the lovely town of Goderich beckon. The Niagara Peninsula, south and east, can easily fill a week-end, with attractions such as Niagara Falls and Ontario's best wine country, charming inns, and award-winning restaurants.

Mennonite horse and buggy, St. Jacobs

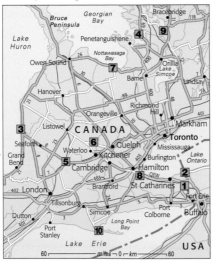

Sights

1. Niagara Falls
2. Niagara-on-the-Lake
3. Goderich
4. Georgian Bay Islands National Park
5. Stratford
6. St. Jacobs and Elora
7. Collingwood
8. Royal Botanical Gardens
9. Gravenhurst
10. Long Point Provincial Park

Queen Street, Niagara-on-the-Lake

Niagara Falls
While the town itself sends kitsch to new heights, the falls are spectacular – truly a natural wonder and well worth the trip *(see pp28–31)*.

Niagara-on-the-Lake
This charming historic town looks much as it did when built in the early to mid-1800s. Beautiful Georgian and Neo-Classical homes and quaint shops reward leisurely exploration. History buffs won't want to miss the Niagara Historical Museum, with exhibits on the region's fascinating past. The town is a good base for excursions along the scenic Niagara Parkway and to excellent wineries *(see p100)*. In summer, it is home to the Shaw Festival. 🗺 *Map Q3 • Niagara Historical Museum: 43 Castlereagh St • 905 468 3912 • Open May–Oct: 10am–5pm daily; Nov–Apr: 1–5pm daily • Adm*

Goderich
Founded in 1827, this town on the shores of Lake Huron has a rich marine history and fine Victorian architecture. Its downtown streets radiate from an unusual octagonal "square," at the center of which is Huron County Courthouse and Courthouse Park. The Huron County Museum has a fine collection of old farm equipment and military artifacts. Other stops of interest include the Huron Historic Gaol (1839–42) and the Marine Museum. 🗺 *Map N2 • Huron County Museum: 110 North St, Open Jan–Apr: 10am–4:30pm Tue–Fri (until 8pm Thu), 1–4:30pm Sat; May–Dec: 10am–4:30pm Tue–Sat (until 8pm Thu), 1–4:30pm Sun • Huron Historic Gaol: 181 Victoria St N, Open May–Aug: 10am–4:30pm Mon–Sat, 1–4:30pm Sun; Sep & Oct: 1–4pm Sun–Fri, 10am–4:30pm Sat, Adm • Marine Museum: Open Jul & Aug: 1–4:30pm daily*

Georgian Bay Islands National Park
Georgian Bay's rugged landscape is characterized by the windswept rock and pine trees of the Canadian Shield. Thousands of islands are scattered across the Bay; 59 make up the park. Access to the largest, Beausoleil, with its hiking trails, sandy beaches, forest, and a variety of reptiles and amphibians, is via a 15-minute boat ride aboard the *DayTripper* from the town of Honey Harbour. 🗺 *Map P1 • DayTripper: 705 526 8907 (reserve ahead)*

Moored boats, Georgian Bay

For information about the Shaw Festival, call 1 800 511 7429, or visit its website at www.shawfest.com

Festival Theatre, Stratford

5 Stratford

Known worldwide for its Shakespeare festival, the city continues the theme of the bard with, among other things, a garden planted with some species named in his plays. Riverside parks are picnic-perfect; shops sell works by local artisans. Check out local history at Stratford-Perth Museum, and a fine example of High Victorian architecture – Perth County Court House (1887). ◈ Map P2

6 St. Jacobs and Elora

Arts and crafts, antiques, and gift shops set in 19th-century buildings; bakeries; and cozy restaurants abound in these historic villages. Craft and food vendors at St. Jacobs' Farmers' Market include those offering the area's specialty, maple syrup, sold by local Mennonites. For more on this sweet treat, visit the Maple Syrup Museum at 1441 King St N, St. Jacobs. A 15-mile (24-km) drive northeast is Elora, on the bank of the Grand River and stunning Elora Gorge. ◈ Map P2 • Farmers' & Flea Market: Farmers' Market Rd, St. Jacobs • Open year-round 7am–3:30pm Thu & Sat and Jun–Labour Day: 8am–3pm Tue

7 Collingwood

This town takes full advantage of Niagara Escarpment scenery. Nearby Blue Mountain, a high point of the escarpment before it dips to Georgian Bay at Collingwood, is Ontario's best ski hill. At Scenic Caves Nature Adventures,

Mennonite Country

St. Jacobs is the heart of Ontario's Old Order Mennonite community. Horse-drawn buggies carrying farmers in dark suits and wide-brimmed black hats, the women in aprons and bonnets, share the road with motor vehicles, and illustrate the way of life of this Anabaptist sect. Shunning modern technology, electricity, and the military, they began settling here in 1799, after immigrating to the US from Europe, where they were persecuted for their beliefs.

walk Ontario's longest suspension footbridge, set high in the treetops, or explore the limestone and ice caves. ◈ Map P1 • Blue Mountain Ski Resort: 705 445 0231 • Scenic Caves Nature Adventures: 705 446 0256

8 Royal Botanical Gardens

Four cultivated gardens and 2,400 acres of nature sanctuaries are replete with greenhouses and trails. In spring, the world's largest lilac collection bursts into bloom. Centuries-old roses thrive summer to fall. In winter, visitors can still enjoy the indoor Mediterranean Garden. Shop, café, and teahouses. ◈ Map P3 • 680 Plains Rd W, Burlington • Open 10am–dusk daily

Maple syrup stand, St. Jacobs Market

Stratford's Shakespeare festival runs April to November; call 1 800 567 1600 or check www.stratfordshakespearefestival.com for details

9 Gravenhurst

The town of Gravenhurst is a good base from which to explore the Muskoka region. It is also the point of departure for lake cruises aboard an 1887 steamship. Stretching from Algonquin Park to Georgian Bay, Muskoka has over 1,600 lakes and rivers. Hundreds of beaches offer swimming opportunities; boats can be rented and outfitters organize canoe trips to secluded areas. Also of interest is Bethune Memorial House, home of Dr Norman Bethune (1890–1939) who advocated for Canadian public health care. ⊗ *Map Q1 • Muskoka Steamships: www.realmuskoka.com • Bethune Memorial House: 235 John St N, Gravenhurst, 705 687 4261, www.pc.gc.ca/bethune*

Lake, Gravenhurst

10 Long Point Provincial Park

This world-renowned refuge for migrating birds has been recognized by the United Nations as a biosphere reserve. Formed over thousands of years by sand washed from Lake Erie's shoreline, the 25-mile (40-km) sand spit has white sand beaches and shallow waters. Spring and fall are excellent for bird-watching; miles of trails through dunes, forests, and wetlands can be enjoyed year-round. Campsites are equipped with showers and electrical hook-up. ⊗ *Map P3 • Hwy 59, 6 miles (10 km) south of Port Rowan • 519 586 2133*

A Drive in the Country

Morning

Start at **St. Jacobs Farmers' and Flea Markets**, admiring the handicrafts, collectibles, and foodstuffs of over 600 vendors. After stocking up on snacks, walk across the parking lot to the **Trolley Shop** for a 75-minute horse-drawn trolley tour through Mennonite farm country (Apr–Oct).

After the tour, drive to the **Visitor Centre** at 1406 King St N; it features a short video on Mennonite history, photo exhibits, and a replica of a Mennonite Meetinghouse. Then, ready for lunch, head to **Stone Crock** (No. 1396), for a country-style buffet.

Afternoon

Drive east on County Road 17; in a few miles you'll come to Road 22. Turn north to Route 86, then east on 86, watching for the sign to **West Montrose**. In this small town, look for the last remaining covered bridge in Ontario – called the kissing bridge by locals. The bridge crosses Grand River, a Heritage Waterway. Take Route 23 (turning into R21) north to charming **Elora**, 10 minutes away.

Once there, browse in the craft and antique shops and admire the old limestone buildings before walking to the **Elora Gorge Conservation Area** to swim, hike, and enjoy your picnic snacks by the water.

Next, it's a short drive on Route 18 to **Fergus**, rich in Scottish history and late 19th-century architecture. Dine at the 1860s **Breadalbane Inn** (487 St. Andrew St W).

Left **Peller Estates Winery** Right **Carriage House, Vineland Estates Winery**

TOP 10 Wineries

1 Vineland Estates Winery
One of the most attractive wineries in the region, this vineyard has an 1857 stone carriage house; an excellent restaurant; and guided tours and tastings. ◈ 3620 Moyer Rd, Vineland • Map Q3 • 1 888 846 3526

2 Peller Estates Winery
Three generations of winemakers are behind this vineyard. Tours include a peek at the barrel-aging cellar. There is also a restaurant and shop. ◈ 290 John St E, Niagara-on-the-Lake • Map Q3 • 1 888 673 5537

3 Trius Winery at Hillebrand
Along with estate tours and tastings, Trius hosts specialty events, such as jazz and blues shows in July and August. ◈ 1249 Niagara Stone Rd, Niagara-on-the-Lake • Map Q3 • 1 800 582 8412

4 Peninsula Ridge Estates Winery
The winemaker, local boy Jamie Evans, creates interesting blends; the whites are especially good. The restaurant (see p101) is set in a lovely Victorian house. ◈ 5600 King St W, Beamsville • Map Q3 • 905 563 0900

5 Inniskillin Wines
One of Ontario's oldest quality vineyards, established in 1975 and famous for its icewines, has guided tours. The shop and tasting bar are in a renovated 1920s barn. ◈ Line 3, Service Rd 66, Niagara-on-the-Lake • Map Q3 • 1 888 466 4754

6 Jackson-Triggs Vinters
This is one of the most technologically advanced facilities in the region. Tours and tastings. ◈ 2145 Niagara Stone Rd, Niagara-on-the-Lake • Map Q3 • 905 468 4637

7 Thirty Bench Wine Makers
This small winery is known for its small lot, limited production wines. Tastings are held in a rustic building overlooking the vineyards. ◈ 4281 Mountainview Rd, Beamsville • Map Q3 • 905 563 1698

8 Malivoire Wine Company
In a region known primarily for its white wines, this organic vineyard produces excellent reds. A tasting room is set amid huge production tanks. ◈ 4260 King St E, Beamsville • Map Q3 • 1 866 644 2244

9 Reif Estate Winery
This family winery has 125 acres (49 ha) of scenic vineyards. The boutique is in a design inspired by an 1870s coach house. Daily tours are held in summer, and visitors can also enjoy the fragrant Wine Sensory Garden. ◈ 15608 Niagara Pkwy, Niagara-on-the-Lake • Map Q3 • 905 468 7738

10 Château des Charmes
This family vineyard boasts over seven generations of wine-growing experience, with grapes harvested exclusively from their vineyards. A tasting bar, shop, and splendid rose garden. ◈ 1025 York Rd, Niagara-on-the-Lake • Map Q3 • 905 262 4219

Some vineyards keep seasonal hours; phone ahead to confirm times. Tasting fees may apply; reservations are recommended

Price Categories

Price categories include	**$** under $30
a three-course meal for	**$$** $30–$50
one, half a bottle of wine,	**$$$** $50–$80
and all unavoidable extra	**$$$$** $80–$110
charges including tax.	**$$$$$** over $110

Above **Rundles**

 # Restaurants

1 Eigensinn Farm
Superstar chef Michael Stadländer creates an unparalleled experience that books up months in advance. Intimately gathered in Stadländer's farmhouse, diners feast on exquisite multiple courses showcasing organic ingredients, many of them from the farm.
◈ RR 2, Singhampton • Map P1 • 519 922 3128 • Bring your own wine • $$$$$

2 Rundles
Classics such as grilled chicken and poached salmon, as well as a more adventurous three-course gourmet menu please at this Stratford institution.
◈ 9 Cobourg St, Stratford • Map P2 • 519 271 6442 • Open May–Oct • $$$$$

3 Bailey's
Casual fine-dining amid small-town charm. The diverse selection of meat, fish, and pasta changes daily. Known for its clam chowder.
◈ 120 Court House Square, Goderich • Map N2 • 519 524 5166 • $$$

4 Langdon Hall
Acclaimed chef Jason Bangerter creates sublime dishes from iconic Canadian ingredients, such as Lake Erie pickerel, and his own kitchen garden bounty. The stately mansion might entice you to stay overnight (see p102).

5 The Church Restaurant
This local institution serves French cuisine in a beautiful old church. Great ambiance and the place to dine if you in the area for the Stratford Festival. Casual, contemporary fare is served upstairs at The Belfry. ◈ 70 Brunswick St, Stratford • Map P2 • 519 273 342 • $$$

6 Tiara
Savory roast and catch of the day join delights such as butter-poached lobster, veal cheeks, and rack-of-lamb on the menu of this upscale hotel restaurant.
◈ 155 Byron St, Niagara-on-the-Lake • Map Q3 • 905 468 2195 • $$$$

7 The Kitchen House at Peninsula Ridge
This restaurant offers fine dining atop a hill in a gorgeous Queen Anne brick home. Part of the Peninsula Ridge Estates Winery (see p100). ◈ 5600 King St W, Beamsville • Map Q3 • 905 563 0900 • $$$$

8 Bijou
Quirky decor sets the stage for imaginative modern French dishes. ◈ 105 Erie St, Stratford • Map P2 • 519 273 5000 • $$$

9 Stone Road Grille
Grille's accomplished and eclectic menu has set it apart in a region brimming with top restaurants. ◈ 238 Mary St, Niagara-on-the-Lake • Map Q3 • 905 468 3474 • $$$$$

10 Peller Estates Winery
Enjoy the enchanting vineyard view and the local, seasonal ingredients used in the five- and seven-course tasting menus.
◈ 290 John St E, Niagara-on-the-Lake • Map Q3 • 1 888 673 5537 • $$$$

Left **Prince of Wales Hotel** Right **Langdon Hall Country House Hotel & Spa**

TOP 10 Country Stays

Prince of Wales Hotel
1 Impeccable service, opulently decorated rooms, a spa, and a wine list to match the fabulous cuisine at this historic hotel in the heart of town. ◈ 6 Picton St, Niagara-on-the-Lake • Map Q3 • 1 888 669 5566 • www.vintage-hotels.com • $$$$

Langdon Hall Country
2 House Hotel & Spa
This country mansion welcomes guests with lovingly tended gardens, well-appointed rooms, a spa, and fine cuisine. ◈ 1 Langdon Dr, RR 3, Cambridge • Map P2 • 1 800 268 1898 • www.langdonhall.ca • $$$$$

The Little Inn at Bayfield
3 This historic inn near Lake Huron, first opened in 1832 as a coach house, justifiably prides itself on its fine restaurant. Country antiques decorate the rooms. Spa. ◈ 26 Main St, Bayfield • Map N2 • 1 800 565 1832 • www.littleinn.com • $$$$

Hockley Valley Resort
4 Nestled in a valley, this is a perfect base for pursuing outdoor activities such as downhill or cross-country skiing, golfing, tennis, and hiking. Spa. ◈ RR 1, Orangeville • Map P2 • 519 942 0754 • www.hockley.com • $$$$

Sherwood Inn
5 On the shores of Lake Joseph, this hotel with cottages makes an ideal base for outdoor pursuits – and weddings. ◈ 1090 Sherwood Rd, Port Carling • Map Q1 • 866 844 2228 • www.sherwoodinn.ca • $$$$

Inn on the Twenty
6 A luxurious inn offering suite accommodations in the heart of Niagara wine country. Spa and winery packages available. ◈ 3845 Main St, Jordan • Map Q3 • 1 800 701 8074 • www.innonthetwenty.com • $$$$

Deerhurst Resort
7 This lakeside resort set on 800 acres (325 ha) of Muskoka countryside, is suitable for both family vacations and quiet getaways. Spa. ◈ 1235 Deerhurst Dr, Huntsville • Map Q1 • 1 800 461 4393 • www.deerhurstresort.com • $$$$$

The Westover Inn
8 Situated in the quiet village of St Marys, this Victorian house was once a seminary. Comfortable rooms and extensive grounds, plus a decent restaurant. ◈ 300 Thomas St, St Mary's • Map P2 • 519 284 2977 • www.westoverinn.com • $$$$

The Oban Inn
9 Overlooking Lake Ontario and surrounded by lush gardens, this inn has beautiful rooms and an excellent restaurant. Short walk to the town center. ◈ 160 Front St, Niagara-on-the-Lake • Map Q3 • 866 359 6226 • www.obaninn.ca • $$$$

Benmiller Inn
10 Close to the beaches of Lake Huron, this inn combines country charm and elegance. Many of the rooms are in an historic wool mill. Spa. ◈ 81175 Benmiller Rd • Map N2 • 1 800 265 1711 • www.benmillerinnandspa.com • $$$$

For hotel price ranges See p115. For more hotels, visit the website www.ontariotravel.net

Left **Handmade straw brooms, St. Jacobs** Right **Jams made from Niagara Peninsula fruits**

Shopping

Farmers' Markets
From June to October, usually on Saturday mornings, local farmers sell fresh produce – fiddleheads, white asparagus, wild blueberries and mushrooms, and much more – at over 148 markets throughout Ontario.
www.farmersmarketsontario.com

Quilts
The best place to buy these durable and gorgeous covers is St. Jacobs, where local Mennonite women still practice the traditional craft of hand-quilting. Be sure to stop in at Grey Fort Quilts.
Grey Fort Quilts: 1425 King St N, St. Jacobs • Map P2 • 1 800 505 2660

Fruits and Preserves
In summer and fall, roadside stands in the Niagara region sell luscious fruits. Local companies turn these fruits into delicious jams, which are available at select stores. Greaves preserves are especially popular. *Greaves Jams and Marmalades: 55 Queen St, Niagara-on-the-Lake • Map Q3 • 1 800 515 9939*

Handmade Furniture
In southern Ontario, especially around Kitchener-Waterloo, Mennonite men craft durable country-style furniture from local woods such as maple and pine. Watch for signs on the smaller roads pointing the way to local carpenters or head to St. Jacobs Furnishings, a large retail outlet.
St. Jacobs Furnishings: 878 Weber St N, St. Jacobs • Map P2 • 519 747 1832

Factory Outlets
Snap up bargains on brands such as Guess, Nine West, and Nike at Niagara Falls' outlet stores, all under one roof, at Canada One.
Canada One: 7500 Lundy's Lane, Niagara Falls • Map Q3 • 905 356 8989

Maple Syrup
The sap of Ontario's sugar maples is made into delicious pancake syrup and candies, sold at farmers' markets and shops.

Arts and Crafts
The work of Ontario's vibrant arts and crafts community, such as pottery, hand-blown glass, and jewelry, can be found thoughout the province at fairs, markets, boutiques, and galleries.

Antiques
Hunting for vintage Canadian furniture, toys, silver, and china in the towns of Ontario is great sport. For a large choice of shops, head to Jordan, St. Jacobs, Erin, Neustadt, and Elora.

Craft-Brewed Beer
Ontario's microbreweries have enjoyed great popularity in recent years. Many, such as Neustadt Springs, offer tastings and tours.
Neustadt Springs: 456 Jacob St, Neustadt • Map P2 • 519 799 5790

Ontario Wines
Sample award-winning wines at vineyards throughout the Niagara Peninsula before stocking up for the home cellar (see p100).

STREETSMART

TORONTO'S TOP 10

Left **Yorkville Park** Right **Nathan Phillips Square, City Hall**

TOP10 Planning Your Trip

1 When to Go
May through October is Toronto's peak tourist season, but the city is a year-round tourist destination. If you like mild, warm weather, visit in spring or early fall. Summer, especially August, is usually hot and humid. In late fall, the temperature drops as the days shorten. Winter months are cold and snowy, suitable for outdoor activities such as skating and indoor pleasures such as theater and shopping. Accommodation rates are lower at this time.

2 What to Pack
Pack a warm sweater and a light jacket in late spring and early fall. In late fall and early spring, pack a heavier jacket or coat and two warm sweaters. In summer, bring a light sweater or blazer, cotton or linen dresses and slacks, and shorts and T-shirts. Sunglasses and sunscreen are a must, as is an umbrella. In winter, pack a hat, scarf, gloves, and warm coat and waterproof boots.

3 Health Insurance
Unless your health insurance covers medical costs while traveling, buying comprehensive health and dental insurance is strongly recommended: Canada does not provide medical services to visitors free of charge. Many credit card companies provide some degree of insurance; it is worthwhile to check this out before your trip.

4 Passports & Visa
A valid passport, combined with a visa when needed, must be presented by visitors upon entry to Canada. Residents of many countries, such as the US, Australia, Ireland, New Zealand, and the majority of European countries, including Britain, do not need a visa to visit Canada. Visitors may remain in Canada for up to six months.

5 Customs
Canada's rules governing what can be brought into the country are complex. In general, do not bring live animals, fresh fruit, vegetables, meat, dairy products, plants, or firearms into Canada without first obtaining authorization. Limited amounts of alcohol and tobacco may be imported duty-free by visitors who are of age (19 and 18 years old, respectively). Upon entry into Canada, you must declare any cash amount equal to or greater than Can$10,000.

6 Driver's License
A driver's license valid in your own country is valid in Ontario for 60 days after you arrive. If you plan to stay longer, an International Driving Permit (obtained in your home country), combined with your license, will allow you to drive in Ontario for up to a year.

7 Car Insurance
Insurance coverage for drivers is mandatory in Ontario; before leaving home, check your own policy to see if you are covered in a rental car. Most rental agencies offer damage and liability insurance; it is a good idea to have both.

8 Electricity
Canada uses a 110-volt, 60-cycle electrical system. Electrical sockets accept two- or three-pronged plugs. Bring a plug adapter and a voltage transformer to run appliances and cellphone chargers that are not manufactured in North America or that don't have an optional voltage switch.

9 Time Zone
Toronto is in the Eastern Standard Time zone (five hours behind Greenwich Mean Time). Daylight Savings Time begins in early March (clocks are turned forward one hour) and ends in early November (clocks are turned back one hour).

10 Discounts
Most movie theaters, major attractions, and public transit offer reduced rates for people over age 65. Students are eligible for many discounts with ID. Hotels also offer discounts *(see p113).*

Contact the Canadian embassy or High Commission nearest you for entry requirements, or visit www.cic.gc.ca/english/visit

Left **Sculpture, Pearson International Airport** Right **Union Station**

TOP10 Arriving in Toronto

1 Pearson International Airport
Terminal 1 services Air Canada and all other Star Alliance airlines, plus a few other airlines. SkyTeam and Oneworld airlines fly out of Terminal 3, as do many other non-affiliated airlines, including Canadian carriers West-Jet and Air Transat. A train connects terminals 1, 3, and a long-stay parking lot. *Flight information: 416 247 7678 or 1 888 207 1690*

2 Immigration
Cards to be filled out for immigration and customs are distributed during international flights. Only one card need be filled out per family. The immigration officer will ask to see your passport or identification papers and may pose additional questions. *1 888 242 2100*

3 Driving from Pearson Airport
The airport is 16 miles (27 km) northwest of downtown Toronto. The trip takes between 20 and 45 minutes, depending on traffic. If renting a car at the airport and driving downtown, take Hwy 427 south to the Gardiner Expressway, then drive east toward the city center, alternatively, take Hwy 409 east to Hwy 27 southbound, which leads to Hwy 427. *Airport Express: 1 800 387 6787*

4 Taxis and buses from Pearson Airport
Taxis (meter) and limousines (flat rate) at the airport are plentiful. TTC's (Toronto Transit Commission) Airport Rocket (route number 192) provides service to all terminals. For downtown destinations, ask the driver for a transfer when boarding. Switch at Kipling Station to the Bloor-Danforth subway. *www.ttc.ca*

5 UPExpress from Pearson Airport
The UPExpress train will shuttle passengers between Pearson Airport and Union Station every 15 minutes from 2015. The journey will take 25 minutes and stop at Weston station, in the northwest of the city, and Bloor station, where visitors can connect to the Bloor-Danforth subway line. Both stations connect to the GO commuter rail lines.

6 Billy Bishop Toronto City Airport
Servicing short haul flights in eastern Canada and the northeast United States, this airport is actually part of the Toronto Islands, and is the main airport for Porter Airlines. Access is via a ferry ride and pedestrian tunnel. A free shuttle bus operates from Union Station. *www.torontoport.com, www.flyporter.com*

7 Car Rental
Most car rental companies have booths at Pearson Airport as well as downtown. Enterprise and Hertz have booths at Billy Bishop Toronto City Airport; some companies are at Union Station. To rent a car you will need a valid credit card and driver's license.

8 Long-Distance Buses
Buses arrive from US and Canada locales at the central bus terminal at 610 Bay St, just north of Dundas. *www.greyhound.ca*

9 By Train
Union Station *(see p66)* is where Amtrak trains arrive from the US and VIA Rail trains pull in from other points in Canada. Commuter-line GO trains also pull-in here. The train station connects to the Union station stop on the north-south subway line; taxis are readily available outside the station.

10 By Car
Highways leading into Toronto are the 401, just north of the city and bringing traffic in from the west and east; the Don Valley Parkway and Hwy 427, running north-south; and the Gardiner Expressway and the Queensway, along Lake Ontario to the south of the city, bringing traffic in from the southwest.

With a few exceptions, you must be over 21 years old to rent a car in Ontario, and some companies do not rent to those under 25

Left **Taxi** Right **Boat tour boarding point, Queen's Quay**

TOP 10 Getting Around Toronto

1 Subway

Toronto's clean and efficient subways are a good way to get around. Free route maps are available at all stations. If you are changing to a bus or streetcar, take a transfer from one of the red dispensers after paying the fare. Transfers are valid for a one-way continuous trip. ✆ *416 393 4636 • 6am–1:30am Mon–Sat, 9am–1am Sun • www.ttc.ca*

2 Buses & Streetcars

Bus and streetcar routes crisscross the city and are well-serviced. Make sure to take a transfer from the driver. You will need it to switch to another route or to the subway, and to provide proof of payment if asked.

3 TTC Fares

Tokens available at TTC (Toronto Transit Commission) stations and shops displaying a "Ticket Agent" sign, are cheaper than a cash fare. Bus and streetcar drivers don't sell tokens nor provide change. You will need the exact fare ($3) if paying by cash. It may be worth buying a day pass, sold at subway stations. ✆ *416 393 4636*

4 Taxis

Flagging a cab on main downtown streets is easy. Rates are set by the city. You can also order a cab over the telephone. ✆ *Beck: 416 751 5555; Co-op: 416 504 2667; Crown: 416 240 0000; Diamond: 416 366 686*

5 Ferries

Ferries to the Toronto Islands depart from the foot of Bay Street, just behind Westin Harbour Castle Hotel. The trip is about 10 minutes. Get to the ferry docks by taking the 510 Spadina streetcar from Union Station to Queens Quay/Ferry Docks station. Note that evening return services are well spaced out. ✆ *Ferry schedules: 416 392 8193*

6 Walking

By foot is the best way to explore the city. Central downtown Toronto streets are fairly safe, even at night. In winter, escape the cold by going underground to the PATH system *(see p25)*

7 Cycling

Cyclists must follow the same rules of the road as drivers. Maps of cycling lanes and paths are available online. The Martin Goodman Trail *(see p94)* is a good alternative to busy streets. Bike theft is a concern in the city; lock up your bike securely when not in use. Wearing a helmet is not mandatory but it is always a good idea; streetcar tracks in particular are a hazard to cyclists. Bikes are allowed on most TTC buses and subways during non-peak hours. ✆ *www.toronto.on.ca/cycling*

8 Bike Sharing

Bike Share Toronto has bicycles parked in the centre of town that can be rented short term and then returned to another bike station. Access to the plan costs an initial fee of $7 for 24 hours or $15 for 72 hours. The first half-hour is then free, followed by $1.50 for up to one hour and $7 for each additional hour. The scheme works out best if you are making numerous short trips. ✆ *www.bikesharetoronto.com*

9 Driving

Toronto's grid system makes driving easy but many streets are one-way. Most major two-way streets forbid left-hand turns during rush hours. Highways are busy during rush hours – especially Hwy 401, Hwy 427, and the Gardiner Expressway – and are best avoided, as is the area around King St and the Gardiner, and Don Valley Parkway. It is illegal to pass a streetcar on the right-hand side when it is stopped to let passengers on or off. Wait 6.5 ft (2 m) behind the rear doors until all the doors have closed.

10 Boat Tours

Several companies offer hour-long tours of Toronto Harbour. You can also book a day tour on a three-masted schooner. All depart from Queen's Quay docks *(see p62)*. ✆ *www.torontoharbour.com*

Note: Children under 2 years travel free on the TTC. Children 2 to 12 years and seniors over 65 years are entitled to reduced rates

Left **Cyclists along the lakefront** Right **Streetcars on Dundas Street**

TOP 10 Toronto on a Budget

1 Free Entertainment

Free entertainment is to be had year-round in Toronto. From Pride Week to dragon boat races, there's an event for everyone (see pp46–7). Throughout the summer, a multitude of free events are held at Harbourfront (see p63), and in late June and early July, jazz festivals keep the fans busy downtown and in The Beach (see p47). There are free celebratory concerts and fireworks on July 1 (Canada Day) and New Year's Eve.
Ⓢ www.toronto.ca/events

2 Parks and Beaches

Whether your taste leans toward roller-blading, walking, playing ball, or sunning yourself, Toronto's parks and beaches (see pp40–41) offer many great ways to relax. Several have excellent sports facilities, as well as grills and picnic tables. Ⓢ www.toronto.ca/parks

3 Cheap Eats

While you can eat fairly cheaply at fast-food chains such as the home-grown Tim Hortons, ethnic restaurants are an excellent alternative. The range of cuisines is astonishing, the prices reasonable (see p81).

4 Free Art

Clustered in Yorkville (see p59) around Hazelton Lane and Cumberland Street, on West Queen West (see p58), and at 25 Morrow Avenue near the Roncesvalles neighborhood (see p39) are galleries selling works by local and international artists. Entry to some public and corporate galleries (see pp34–5) is free. The outdoor public art is also worth checking out (see p37).

5 Free Tours

Heritage Toronto gives free walking tours in summer, covering such diverse topics as the city's railroad history or its water supply. Book ahead or just show up. Ⓢ 416 338 0684 • mid-Jun–mid-Oct • www.heritagetoronto.org

6 Package Deals

Tourism Toronto offers packages for short stays for visitors throughout the year. The deals serve to promote hotels, restaurants, and the city's numerous attractions. Ⓢ www.seetorontonow.com

7 CityPass

This pass is available online and payable in US dollars or in Canadian funds at the ticket booth of the attractions featured: Casa Loma (see pp18–19), CN Tower (see pp12–13), Royal Ontario Museum (see pp8–11), Ontario Science Centre (see p34), and Toronto Zoo (see p91). CityPass offers substantial discounts on admission – amounting to 45 percent if you visit all participating sights. It is valid for nine days from your first sight visit. Ⓢ www.citypass.com

8 Transit Savings

Single day passes, valid weekdays, are available at all subway stations. A day pass covers you on a weekday until 5am the next day. The same pass covers two adults and up to four children on a Saturday, Sunday, or public holiday until 5am the next day. These passes offer real savings. Monthly passes and passes for convention visitors are also available. Ⓢ 416 393 4636 • www.ttc.ca

9 Free Admission Days

Some city attractions, such as the Royal Ontario Museum (see pp8–11) and Art Gallery of Ontario (see pp16–17), offer one free day or evening per week. Bear in mind that although cheaper, the crowds can be greater.

10 Hotel Savings

Many hotels offer discounts when booked online. If booking directly or through an agent, don't forget to ask about discounts. If you go for a non-refundable rate, most hotels will offer a discount of around 15 to 20 percent. Members of auto clubs and AARP (American Association of Retired Persons) often qualify for discounts.

Harbourfront hosts free concerts, readings, festivals, and more year-round; visit its website at www.harbourfrontcentre.com

109

Left **Bell phones** Right **Wheelchair access sign**

Useful Information

Drinking
The legal drinking age in Ontario is 19. Ontario has strict laws about drinking in public: open bottles of alcohol are not allowed in public places. Fenced-off areas are set aside for selling and consuming alcohol at large events.

Media
The two largest Canadian newspapers are produced in Toronto: The *Globe and Mail* and the *Toronto Star*, along with a daily tabloid, *Toronto Sun*. Popular radio stations include CBC Radio One (FM 99.1) for news, CBC Radio Two (FM 92.1) for classical music, JazzFM91 (FM 91.1) for jazz, CHFI (FM 98.1) for easy-listening music, CHUM (FM 104.5) and Q107 (FM 107.5) for rock music. The most popular Canadian TV stations are CBC, CTV, GLOBAL, BRAVO and CityTV, and, in Ontario, TVO.

Entertainment Listings
Toronto weekly *Now* is available for free at cafés, bars, bookshops, libraries, and street boxes throughout the city and is the best source for information on the local music and art scene. The monthly magazine *Toronto Life* is also helpful. These listings are also online. ⑨ *www. torontolife.com*

Currency
The Canadian unit of currency is the dollar, which is divided into 100 cents. Coins come in denominations of 5, 10, and 25 cents, and 1 and 2 dollars. Bank notes (bills) come in denominations of $5, $10, $20, $50, $100, and $500. Plan to arrive with at least $50 to $100 in local currency and acquire change as soon as you can for tips and travel.

Taxes
In Canada, taxes are not included in the listed price unless specified, so when making a purchase reckon with a further 13 percent with HST (harmonized sales tax). ⑨ *www. cra-arc.gc.ca*

Websites
Extensive information on the city of Toronto and the province of Ontario is available on the Internet.
⑨ *www.toronto.ca*
• *www.ontariotravel.net*
• *www.seetorontonow.com*

Telephones
Public telephones are often both coin and card operated. Local calls cost $0.50; directory assistance (411) is free. Post offices, most convenience stores, and specially marked Bell machines sell phone cards. Within Toronto you must prefix the local telephone number with either of the area codes 417 or 647, or with 905 for calls to Greater Toronto (note some 905 numbers are

long distance and require the prefix 1). For a long-distance number in North America, dial the prefix 1 and then the city code. To dial abroad, dial 011 + country code + city code (dropping any 0).

Public Holidays
New Year's Day (Jan 1), Family Day (3rd Mon in Feb), Good Friday and Easter Monday (Mar or Apr), Victoria Day (usually 3rd Mon in May), Canada Day (Jul 1), civic holiday (1st Mon in Aug), Labour Day (1st Mon in Sep), Thanksgiving (2nd Mon in Oct), Christmas Day (Dec 25), Boxing Day (Dec 26). Remembrance Day (Nov 11) is a holiday for banks and government offices.

Disabled Visitors
Bathrooms in older buildings are located up or down stairs and are not easily accessible; large entertainment venues are. In 2014, the TTC introduced the first wheelchair accessible streetcars to the Spadina route 510. The new streetcars will be rolled out on all routes by 2019. The subway is also becoming more accessible, with more elevators to platforms and fully accessible ticket gates.

Consulates
In emergencies, your consulate may give assistance. ⑨ UK: 777 Bay St, Map K3, 416 593 1267
• US: 360 University Ave, Map K2, 416 595 1700

Left **Hospital sign** Center **Police car** Right **No smoking sign**

Security & Health

1 Theft Prevention

Pickpockets are present in all large cities, especially in crowded places. Pay attention to your surroundings and avoid being distracted, especially if someone bumps into you. Don't carry more cash with you than you need and don't carry your wallet in a back pocket. If you have a purse, ensure it closes tightly. Always watch your luggage carefully at airports, at bus and train stations, and when checking in and out of your hotel. Leave valuables in the hotel's safe.

2 Hotel Room Safety

When you've checked into your room, look on the back of the entrance door for a map showing the escape route to take in case of fire. Always leave the security latch in place when in your room and don't admit strangers. Some hotels have floors for women-only – ask when booking, if you are a woman traveling alone.

3 Food Safety

Any establishment in Toronto that serves food, including pubs and delicatessens, are inspected regularly by city health officials. The green, yellow, or red card hanging in the window reflects the overall mark given on conditions such as cleanliness. Green denotes a full pass, yellow a conditional pass, red a failure.

4 Telephone Helplines

Various helplines are available to call in a crisis.
§ *Emergency: 911*
• *Toronto Police Services: 416 808 2222* • *Kids Help Phone: 1 800 668 6868*
• *Assaulted Women's Help Line: 416 863 0511*
• *Distress Centre of Toronto: 416 408 4357*
• *Poison Control: 416 813 5900* • *Telehealth Ontario: 1 866 797 0000*

5 Public Transit

Always look to your right to make sure no cars are coming before exiting a streetcar. Subway platforms provide designated waiting areas; these are recommended at night. Available on TTC buses, Request Stop allows a woman to get off a bus at locations between regular TTC stops. Tell the driver at least one stop ahead of where you want to get off and leave the bus by the front doors. The rear doors will remain closed so that no one can follow you off.

6 Knowing Your Surroundings

Avoid dark places at night, especially if you are on your own. Carry a good map with you and check out the route to and from your destination before starting out. If you plan on returning late, make sure you have enough change and cash to call for and pay for a taxi.

7 Hospital Emergency Rooms

Emergency treatment is available 24 hours a day.
§ *St Michael's: 30 Bond St, Map L3, 416 360 4000*
• *Toronto General: 200 Elizabeth St, Map K2, 416 340 3946* • *Mt Sinai: 600 University Ave, Map K2, 416 586 5054* • *Hospital for Sick Children: 555 University Ave, Map K2, 416 813 1500* • *Toronto East General: 825 Coxwell St, Map B2, 416 461 8272*

8 Dental Emergencies

An emergency referral service, the Academy of Dentistry, links you with a nearby dentist after regular office hours. After midnight, go to a hospital emergency room. § *Academy of Dentistry: 416 967 5649*

9 Smoking

Toronto is a smoke-free city except in designated areas. All public spaces are smoke-free and smoking is outlawed in vehicles carrying passengers under 16 years.

10 Pharmacies

The majority of pharmacies are open from 9am to 9 or 10pm and many are open until later. Some Shoppers Drug Mart pharmacies are 24-hour. One of the most central is at Yonge and Carlton. § *Shoppers Drug Mart: 465 Yonge St, Map L2, 416 408 4000 or 1 800 746 7737*

Left **The Colonnade, Bloor Street West** Right **Vintage clothing store, Kensington Market**

🔟 Shopping Tips

1 Store Hours
Most shops are open 10am to 6pm, Monday to Saturday (often later on Thursday and Friday). Department stores and shops in malls and commercial districts may keep longer hours, from 10am to 9pm, Monday to Saturday, and from noon to 5pm on Sunday. Widely observed retail holidays are Christmas, January 1, July 1, Labour Day, and Thanksgiving.

2 Payment
MasterCard, American Express, and Visa credit cards are widely accepted, Diner's Club and Discovery less so. Bank debit cards compatible with the Interac, Plus, or Cirrus systems are also widely accepted. You will need your PIN.

3 Sales & Returns
Look for end-of-season savings on merchandise. Excellent savings are to be had on Boxing Day (December 26), when prices at many stores are reduced dramatically. Discounted items (and sometimes even those at full price) may not be returnable, or may be exchanged only, or be within a certain time period. Be sure to ask about the return policy before making a purchase.

4 Department Stores
Canada's largest department store chain, The Bay (see p25), carries practically everything.

The branch at Queen stocks high-end and brand name clothes and has a massive and very fashionable shoe section. The smaller Holt Renfrew (see p77) sells high-end clothing and accessories while Drake General Store (see p78) is packed full of cool gifts, from retro CBC tees (Canadian Broadcasting Corporation) and Mountie coasters, to rustic tin cups. A branch of the famous luxury department store Saks Fifth Avenue shares space with Drake General Store.

5 Shopping Malls
The largest downtown mall is Eaton Centre (see pp24–5). Other malls are Queen's Quay Terminal (see p63), ManuLife Centre, College Park, and the network of malls on the PATH system (see p25). ⓢ College Park: 444 Yonge St • Map L2

6 Music
For local flavor and good prices, visit Soundscapes. Classical and jazz lovers should head to L'Atelier Grigorian (see p77). For vinyl, there's Kops Records. ⓢ Kops Records: 229 Queen St W, Map J4 • Soundscapes: 572 College St, Map K2

7 Books
Book City has a good selection and a number of locations. The big

Canadian chain Indigo sells much beyond books but still has a reasonable book section. Other excellent bookshops are Type (see p78) for fiction, art and design, Open Air Books & Maps for maps and travel guides, Ben McNally Books for fiction in particular, and Bakka-Phoenix Books for science fiction. ⓢ Bakka-Phoenix Books: 84 Harbord St, Map C3 • Ben McNally Books: 366 Bay St, Map K4 • Book City: 348 Danforth Ave, Map F3 • Indigo: 55 Bloor St W, Map D3 • Open Air Books & Maps: 25 Toronto St, Map L4

8 Alcohol
Sales of alcohol are restricted to LCBO (Liquor Control Board of Ontario) outlets (wine, spirits, and beer), the Beer Store (beer and coolers), and a few small wine stores. ⓢ www.lcbo.com, 1 800 668 5226 • www.the beerstore.ca

9 Convenience Stores
Small shops selling cigarettes, toiletry necessities, cold drinks, snacks and fresh produce, and lottery tickets are ubiquitous in Toronto. Many stores also sell transit tokens.

10 Untaxed Goods
Books and groceries are exempt from the 13 percent HST (harmonized sales tax). There is no visitor rebate scheme.

The shopping malls Queen's Quay Terminal **See p63** and Toronto Eaton Centre **See pp24–5** are open on some public holidays

Left **Hot dog cart** Right **Entrance, Royal Meridien King Edward Hotel**

TOP 10 Accommodation & Dining Tips

1 Hotel Taxes
In Ontario, accommodation is taxed with a 13 percent HST (harmonized sales tax). An additional 3 percent destination tax is also levied on some hotel rooms in the City of Toronto.

2 Rooms
In general, hotel rooms are well furnished and of a fairly good size. Most have two double beds or one queen- or king-sized bed; standard twin-bedded rooms may also be available. If you are sensitive to noise, ask for a room away from the elevator and the ice and dispensing machines; if you are sensitive to smoke, ask for a smoke-free room.

3 Rack Rates
Hotel rates vary according to the hotel category, and the day of the week and season. Peak rates are weekdays and from April to December. Rack rates, the basic room rates, are the ones used in this book to provide a guide price. It is almost always possible to get a better deal, especially if you book online. Also, discounts are often available to members of clubs such as automobile associations or the Elderhostel. When booking, ask what special rates apply and make sure to bring proof of membership with you (see p109).

4 Concierges
Mid- and large-size hotels have concierges on staff whose job it is to cater to the needs and whims of the guests. They will procure tickets to shows and sports games, make restaurant reservations, arrange transportation, and offer helpful tips.

5 Extra Costs
Parking at downtown hotels is almost always extra, paid on a per-night basis. Telephone calls made from your in-room phone can be expensive, as can drinks and snacks consumed from the room's minibar. Note that many hotels also charge for WiFi.

6 Restaurant Reservations
Most restaurants take reservations and it is a good idea to book a table at a popular dining spot well in advance of your trip. Mention if you have special needs or dietary requirements. It is considered good form to cancel your reservation if your plans change.

7 Tipping
Tips and service charges are not usually added to dining bills. For service at restaurants, cafés, and clubs, plan on tipping about 15 percent of the pre-tax amount. An easy way of estimating the tip is to add up the taxes on the bill. At bars, leave a dollar or two for the bartender. Tip porters and bellhops at least $1 per bag or suitcase; cloakroom attendants, $1 per garment; and chambermaids, a minimum of $1 to $2 per day. A hotel doorman will also appreciate a dollar or two for his services.

8 Dress Codes
Jacket and tie are almost never required in restaurants, though many diners opt to wear them on a special evening out, especially to an upscale place. Some clubs, however, may not allow you in if you are wearing sneakers or jeans.

9 Cellphones
At most restaurants, it is considered quite uncourteous to leave your cellphone turned on or to carry on cellphone conversations inside.

10 Meal Times
Breakfast is usually served in diners and coffee shops from about 6am to 10am. Lunch is available from about 11:30am to 2pm, dinner between about 5pm and 10pm. Many restaurants and pubs offer a late-night menu. Brunches are often served on weekends only – and at some spots, on Sundays only – usually from 11am–2pm or later. Some clubs are closed on Sundays or Mondays, while others are closed on both days – call ahead to check.

Left **Madison Manor** Right **Suite, Roehampton Hotel**

🔟 Inexpensive Hotels

1 Bond Place Hotel
Ideally located in the heart of downtown Toronto, this hotel is close to the Toronto Eaton Centre, the theater district, and other local attractions. Rooms are modern and well-equipped, and the hotel has a restaurant. ⊗ *65 Dundas St E • Map D4 • 416 362 6061 • www. bondplace.ca • $$$*

2 Hotel Victoria
Just steps from Union Station in the city's Financial District, this small hotel, with just 56 rooms, offers all the amenities of a large hotel, along with excellent service. It is close to many top attractions. ⊗ *56 Yonge St • Map L4 • 416 363 1666 • www.hotelvictoria-toronto. com • $$$*

3 Madison Manor
Featuring many unusual details, including fireplaces and alcove windows, the owners of this lovingly restored Victorian mansion aim to make guests feel as though they have stepped into an English country inn. To further the illusion, there's a pub next door. ⊗ *20 Madison Ave • Map C3 • 416 922 5579 • www.madisonmanor boutiquehotel.com • $$*

4 Hotel Ocho
You couldn't ask for a better location than this converted garment factory in Chinatown – it's steps to everything. Distressed white-washed walls and dark wood furniture in the stylish rooms. ⊗ *195 Spadina Ave • Map H3 • 416 593 0885 • www. hotelocho.com • $$$$*

5 Canadas Best Value Hotel Toronto
At the intersection of the 427 and the Gardiner Expressway, this clean and comfortable chain-hotel is located on the outer fringes of central Toronto, on one of the routes from Pearson Airport. ⊗ *650 Evans Ave • Map A2 • 416 255 5500 • www.canadasbestvalue-inn.com • $$*

6 Canadiana Backpackers Inn
Amazing central location at this friendly hostel split over ten adjoining Victorian houses. Pancake breakfast thrown in Mon to Thu and bagels on the weekends. There are discounts available for Hostel International members and ISIC card holders) ⊗ *42 Widmer St • Map J4 • 416 598 9090 • www.canadianalodging. com • $*

7 The Strathcona Hotel
Guests enjoy the modern, updated rooms (including that rare type – a single), and can use a fitness club next door. The hotel is right by the Air Canada Centre and close to other major attractions; a pub and restaurant are located in the hotel. ⊗ *60 York St • Map K4 • 416 363 3321 • www. thestrathconahotel.com • $$$*

8 Roehampton Hotel and Suites
With its heated rooftop pool and well-appointed rooms and suites, this Best Western is a pleasant, affordable home away from home. It is a short walk to the Eglinton subway station and the many excellent shops and restaurants nearby. ⊗ *808 Mt Pleasant Rd • Map B2 • 416 487 5101 • www.bestwestern. com • $$$*

9 Travelodge Toronto Airport
Reasonably priced accommodation with comfortable rooms. The hotel is situated a very short drive from Pearson International Airport. Indoor pool and free airport shuttle service. ⊗ *925 Dixon Rd • Map A1 • 416 674 2222 • www. travelodgetorontoairport.ca • $$*

10 Gladstone Hotel
The unique, artist-designed rooms at this trendy, welcoming hotel are compact but comfortable. The Gladstone hosts arts events, and has a lively bar and café, but it can be noisy. ⊗ *1214 Queen St W • Map K4 • 416 531 4635 • www.glad stonehotel.com • $$$$*

Price Categories

For a standard, double room per night (with breakfast if included), taxes and extra charges.

$	under $100
$$	$100–150
$$$	$150–200
$$$$	$200–300
$$$$$	over $300

Above **Pool, The Grand**

TOP 10 Mid-priced Hotels

1 Hyatt Regency Toronto

The extensively renovated Hyatt is just a step away from the city's entertainment district. Rooms overlook downtown and Lake Ontario. ❧ *370 King St W • Map J4 • 416 343 1234 • www.torontoregency. hyatt.com • $$$$*

2 Novotel Toronto Centre

Well-placed near many downtown attractions, this hotel is a good representative of the French chain. The large rooms are functional, and there is a lovely lobby, a fitness room, and indoor pool. ❧ *45 The Esplanade • Map L5 • 416 367 8900 • www. novotel.com • $$$$*

3 International Plaza Hotel

This hotel located near Pearson Airport has 433 exceptionally well-appointed guestrooms and is a popular conference center. A variety of restaurants and cafés, along with a spa, a modern fitness centre, and an indoor swimming pool with water slides, and a hot tub, ensure you rarely need leave the premises. ❧ *655 Dixon Rd • Map A2 • 416 244 1711 • www.internationalplaza hotel.com • $$$*

4 Courtyard Toronto Downtown

An indoor pool, exercise room, and hot tub are among the amenities

found in this comfortable 17-floor Marriott hotel. With many high-tech conveniences in the rooms, such as wireless Internet, a working stay here is enjoyable. ❧ *475 Yonge St • Map L2 • 416 924 0611 • www. marriott.com • $$$*

5 The Grand

Rooms and suites in this large hotel are spacious and luxuriously furnished; some have private terraces. Features include an opulent pool, a huge rooftop patio with two whirlpools and spectacular city views, a spa and fitness club, a business center, and meeting rooms. ❧ *225 Jarvis St • Map M3 • 416 863 9000 • www.grandhotel toronto.com • $$$$*

6 Radisson Plaza Hotel Admiral Toronto Harbourfront

Bright, large rooms in this hotel, steps from Lake Ontario and harbourfront attractions. The hotel appeals to both business and leisure travelers alike. There is a good restaurant, and a rooftop pool and deck overlooking the lake. ❧ *294 Queens Quay W • Map J6 • 416 203 3333 • www.radisson.com • $$$$*

7 Marriott Gateway on the Falls

The east-facing rooms in this comfortable high-rise hotel offer fantastic views of Niagara Falls.

The hotel staff are extremely knowledgable and helpful and the rooms are large and well-appointed. ❧ *6755 Fallsview Blvd, Niagara Falls • Map Q3 • 1 800 618 9059 • www.marriott.com • $$*

8 Hôtel le Germain Maple Leaf Square

Boutique lodgings in a modern built enclave by the Air Canada Centre. ❧ *75 Bremner Blvd • Map K5 • 416 649 7575 • www. germainmapleleafsquare. com • $$$$$*

9 Eaton Chelsea

The biggest hotel in Canada, with 1,590 guest rooms, The Eaton Chelsea caters equally well to business travelers and families. An indoor waterslide, a kids center, and a teen lounge with X Boxes, and a pool table go a long way to keeping all ages amused. ❧ *33 Gerrard St W • Map L2 • 416 595 1975 • www. eatonhotels.com • $$$*

10 Cambridge Suites

Excellent service is standard at this hotel offering two-room suites only. The fully equipped work areas have all the bells and whistles. A microwave, fridge, and coffeemaker in every suite ensure you have all you need for a comfortable stay. ❧ *15 Richmond St E • Map L4 • 416 368 1990 • www.cambridge-suitestoronto.com • $$$$*

For accommodation outside Toronto See p102

Left **Fairmont Royal York** Right **Hotel Le Germain**

TOP 10 Luxury & Boutique Hotels

1 Soho Metropolitan
Lovers of luxury adore this boutique hotel in the Entertainment District. Duvets, walk-in closets, extravagant bathrooms with heated marble floors, and many high-tech gadgets are standard. Luckee, a nouvelle chinois restaurant, is on the ground floor (see p69). 🅂 318 Wellington St W • Map J4 • 416 599 8800 • www.metropolitan.com/soho • $$$$$

2 The Omni King Edward Hotel
Opened in 1903, this grand historic hotel, affectionately called "the King Eddy", offers elegantly appointed rooms, courteous service, spa, and every possible amenity; guests want for nothing. 🅂 37 King St E • Map L4 • 416 863 9700 • www.omnihotels.com/toronto • $$$$

3 Trump Hotel
The 65-story Trump Tower raises the luxury bar in the heart of the city, with a spa, a fitness center, fine dining downstairs, and superfast broadband. 🅂 325 Bay St • Map L4 • 416 214 2800 • www.trumphotelcollection/toronto • $$$$$

4 The Hazelton
A favorite with jet-setters, Toronto's first five-star hotel is located in the heart of Yorkville. It boasts glamorous Hollywood-style rooms

and the city's best celebrity-spotting bar. 🅂 118 Yorkville Ave • Map C3 • 416 963 6300 • www.thehazeltonhotel.com • $$$$$

5 Park Hyatt Toronto
Luxurious, spacious rooms with marble bathrooms and free high-speed Internet access, attentive service, and a central Yorkville location, make this classy hotel a great favorite. The Roof Lounge (see p56) provides a spectacular view of the city, and its posh Stillwater Spa is one of the city's best. 🅂 4 Avenue Rd • Map C3 • 416 925 1234 • www.parktoronto/hyatt.com • $$$$$

6 Fairmont Royal York
Across from Union Station, this large hotel has been a Toronto landmark since 1929. The magnificent lobby is a fitting backdrop for the many heads of state who have stayed here. There are several restaurants and bars, including the cozy Library Bar (see p67), and a great spa. 🅂 100 Front St W • Map K5 • 416 368 2511 • www.fairmont.com/royalyork • $$$$

7 Hôtel le Germain
With its modern, understated decor, this boutique hotel is the very height of elegance. Its mission – to promote

relaxation while pampering its guests with luxury – succeeds every time. 🅂 30 Mercer St • Map J4 • 416 345 9500 • www.germaintoronto.com • $$$$$

8 Windsor Arms
Personal service is writ large in this elegant hotel with just 28 guest rooms, located on the first four floors of a 14-story building. Guests enjoy the two-floor spa and delight in the cuisine of Courtyard Café (see p54). There's also a steakhouse, lounge, and tearoom. 🅂 18 Thomas St • Map C3 • 416 971 9666 • www.windsorarmshotel.com • $$$$$

9 The Old Mill Inn
This inn on the Humber River is a 15-minute drive west of downtown. All 44 rooms overlook the river; the 13 suites are located in the historic old mill building. Rooms are luxurious and there's an excellent restaurant, spa, and wellness center. 🅂 21 Old Mill Rd • Map A2 • 416 236 2641 • www.oldmilltoronto.com • $$$$$

10 Shangri-la Hotel
This luxury hotel spans 17 floors and has a distinctly Asian aesthetic – raw silk wall coverings, tea libraries, and a patio with a Japanese garden. Rooms are smart and modern. 🅂 188 University Ave • Map K4 • 647 788 8888 • www.shangri-la.com/toronto • $$$$$

➔ *Note: Unless otherwise stated, all hotels accept credit cards and have private bathrooms and air conditioning*

Above **Lobby, Double Tree by Hilton Hotel Toronto Downtown**

🔟 Business-Friendly Hotels

1 Hilton Toronto
Centrally located in the financial district, this Hilton is geared to businesspeople. Standard rooms are spacious, suites ideal for longer stays, and executive rooms provide extras such as special work chairs. ◎ *145 Richmond St W • Map K4 • 416 869 3456 • www.hilton. com • $$$$*

2 Westin Harbour Castle
With a location on Lake Ontario, yet close to downtown, this high-rise hotel offers stunning views from its ample rooms. Facilities include a pool, fitness room, outdoor tennis court, spacious meeting rooms, and full business service. ◎ *1 Harbour Sq • Map K6 • 416 869 1600 • www. westin.com/harbourcastle • $$$$*

3 Toronto Marriott Airport
Convenient for Pearson Airport, 405 rooms in this Marriott are designed for the business traveler. All rooms have high-speed Internet access. Meeting rooms are plentiful, and an indoor pool and health club help shed the stress. ◎ *901 Dixon Rd • Map A2 • 416 674 9400 • www. marriott.com • $$$$*

4 Sheraton Centre
Steps from City Hall, this hotel complex bustles year-round with conventioneers and tour groups.

There are 1,377 rooms and good, efficient service. ◎ *123 Queen St W • Map K4 • 416 361 1000 • www. sheratontoronto.com • $$$$*

5 InterContinental Toronto Centre
Attached to the Convention Centre, this hotel provides attentive service and excellent business facilities. The eighth floor is reserved for Priority Club business guests. ◎ *225 Front St W • Map J5 • 416 597 1400 • www.torontocentre.inter continental.com • $$$$*

6 The Suites at One King West
Located in Toronto's Financial District, this hotel is uniquely built atop an historic 1914 building that once housed the Dominion Bank of Canada. The hotel boasts a 24-hour business center, bistro, and private club. The views are breathtaking. ◎ *1 King St W • Map K4 • 416 548 8100 • www. onekingwest.com • $$$*

7 The Westin Bristol Place Toronto Airport
Five minutes from Pearson Airport, the hotel surprises at check-in with a waterfall in its lobby. Guests appreciate the modern, spacious rooms, personalized service, fitness center, indoor pool, and other amenities. ◎ *950 Dixon Rd • Map A2*

• *416 675 9444 • www. westintorontoairport.com • $$$*

8 Double Tree by Hilton Hotel Toronto Downtown
Elegant contemporary decor and luxurious touches such as down duvets pamper travelers. Two award-winning restaurants, Hemispheres and Lai Wah Heen (see p53), add to the pleasure of a stay here. ◎ *108 Chestnut St • Map K3 • 416 977 5000 • http:// doubletree3.hilton.com • $$$$*

9 Toronto Marriott Downtown Eaton Centre
Featuring a full business center with secretarial service, dedicated business guestrooms, and 18 meeting rooms, this 18-story hotel is conveniently located beside the Toronto Eaton Centre (see pp24–5). ◎ *525 Bay St • Map K3 • 416 597 9200 • www.marriott.com • $$$$$*

10 Westin Prince Toronto
Set in a large park northeast of downtown, this hotel is an oasis of comfort. Its several bars and restaurants – including Katsura (see p95) – handsome rooms, and a business center explain this hotel's popularity. ◎ *900 York Mills Rd • Map B1 • 416 444 2511 • www. westin.com/prince • $$$*

Left **By the Park Bed & Breakfast** Right **House on McGill**

TOP 10 Bed & Breakfasts

1 Suite Dreams B&B
At the west end of the Annex, in an area sometimes dubbed Korea Town and just a block from Christie subway, this B&B offers four spacious rooms with attached bathrooms. There's a two-night minimum stay. Superb value. 🅢 *390 Clinton St • Map B3 • 416 538 0417 • www.suite dreamstoronto.com • $$$*

2 Jare's Place
Get into Leslieville living, at this colorful three-bedroom B&B. Thoughtful touches such as handmade soaps and cloth shopping bags for guests to borrow, add to the welcoming feel. Great breakfasts. 🅢 *87 Empire Ave • Map F4 • 416 778 1940 • www.jareplace. ca • $$*

3 Pimblett's Downtown Toronto B&B
Five cozy rooms in a Victorian house decorated to the nines with all things British, from antiques to bric-a-brac, offer an unforgettably eccentric stay in Cabbagetown. Geoffrey Pimblett, the owner, amuses guests with take-offs of the Queen of England. 🅢 *242 Gerrard St E • Map E4 • 416 921 6898 • www.pimblett.ca • $$*

4 Smiley's B&B
Snuggle-up in the roof-top Belvedere Room of this Algonquin Island cottage. Breakfast with your hosts, appreciate the tranquility, and explore the Toronto Islands. A studio that sleeps four is available in summer. 🅢 *4 Dacotah Ave • Map D6 • 416 203 8599 • www. eralda.ca • $$–$$$*

5 Annex Garden B&B
Stay in a huge historic house in an unbeatable location in Little Italy. Two rooms and two apartments are available in this spiffy home with four fireplaces and under-floor heating.🅢 *Euclid Ave • Map B3 • 416 258 1179 • www.annexgarden.com • $$$$*

6 Making Waves Boatel
Be lulled to sleep by the lap of Lake Ontario. Right in the Harbourfront marina, this moored boat has two tiny cabin rooms with a shared bath, and a larger Bondi Stateroom with private bathroom. Enjoy evening drinks under the stars on the Sky Lounge. 🅢 *539 Queens Quay W • Map H6 • 647 403 2764 • www. boatel.ca • $$$$*

7 Au Petit Paris
Just east of downtown and within a 15-minute walk of the upscale shops on Bloor Street and in Yorkville, this B&B has a Paris flair. Its four rooms, all with private baths, are in shades of ochre and red. Breakfast is served in the dining room or on the rooftop patio. 🅢 *3 Selby St • Map D3 • 416 928 1348 • www.bbtoronto. com/aupetitparis • $$*

8 By the Park Bed & Breakfast
In this lovingly restored 1910 home, rooms are large and bathrooms are luxurious. Depending on the season, guests can unwind in the beautiful garden or warm up by one of the fireplaces. Includes a delicious home-cooked vegan or vegetarian breakfast. 🅢 *92 Indian Grove • Map A2 • 416 520 6102 • www. bythepark.ca • $$*

9 Banting House Inn
Seven rooms thoughtfully refurbished with bright blocks of color and Canadian themes. A few blocks from the Gay Village, or in the opposite direction, Cabbagetown. 🅢 *73 Homewood Ave • Map M1 • 416 924 1458 • www. bantinghouseinn.com • $$$*

10 House on McGill
Eight tastefully decorated rooms, some with shared baths, and reasonable prices make this B&B in a restored Victorian townhouse a good choice for the budget-conscious traveler. It is centrally located, about a 10-minute walk from the Eaton Centre. 🅢 *110 McGill St • Map L2 • 416 351 1503 • $$*

Price Categories

For a standard, double room per night (with breakfast if included), taxes and extra charges.

$	under $100
$$	$100–150
$$$	$150–200
$$$$	$200–300
$$$$$	over $300

Above **Hostelling International Toronto**

Budget Accommodation

Annex Quest House

With its dark pine furnishings, natural decor, vibrant colors, and tastefully appointed guest rooms dedicated to one of the four elements – earth, fire, air, and water – travelers will enjoy the calming atmosphere of this retreat from the city. Located near Casa Loma. ✆ *83 Spadina Rd • Map C2 • 416 922 1934 • www.annexquesthouse. com • $$*

Quality Hotel & Suites Airport East

In the west of the city, near Pearson Airport and major traffic arteries, this hotel has large, comfortable standard rooms and suites. Extra features include free parking and airport shuttle service running from 3am to 11pm. ✆ *2180 Islington Ave • Map A2 • 416 240 9090 • www.choicehotels.ca • $*

Victoria University

Located on the University of Toronto campus, Victoria University opens its doors to budget-minded travelers during summer-semester holidays, mid-May to the end of August. A quiet setting combined with a central location make these lodgings an excellent base from which to explore the city. ✆ *140 Charles St W • Map D3 • 416 585 4524 • www. vicu.utoronto.ca • $*

Neill-Wycik College Hotel

This student residence turns into a guest house from early May to the end of August. While the rooms are spartan and bathrooms are shared, the price is right for tight budgets. Groups are welcome. The central location means many of the city's top destinations are in walking distance. Breakfast is included. ✆ *96 Gerrard St E • Map M2 • 416 977 2320 • www. neill-wycik.com • $*

Victoria's Mansion Inn and Guest House

In the heart of Toronto's Gay and Lesbian Village on a tree-lined street, this charming small hotel, with a lovely Victorian-style garden, provides a respite from the bustle of the city. All rooms come with private baths, and suites are equipped with a fridge and microwave. Free parking. ✆ *68 Gloucester St • Map L1 • 416 921 4625 • www. victoriasmansion.com • $$*

Super 8 Downtown

If your priority is a central location, consider the Super 8 right in the middle of Chinatown, steps from Kensington Market and Queen West. Accommodations are basic. Breakfast is included. ✆ *222 Spadina Ave • Map H3 • 647 426 8118 • www. super8.com • $$$*

Days Inn Toronto East Beaches

A basic chain hotel, but well located for wandering The Beach neighborhood along Queen East. Good places for brunch and Leslieville's vintage stores are nearby too. ✆ *1684 Queen St E • 416 694 1177 • www.daysinn.ca • $$$*

ALT Hotel Toronto Airport

This concept hotel is located on the airport site at the end of the LINK train line. Contemporary rooms are smartly designed. ✆ *6080 Viscount Rd • Map A2 • 905 362 4337 • www.toronto.alt hotels.ca • $$$*

Hostelling International Toronto

Offering mainly shared rooms in dorms, a stay here is one of the cheapest in the city. Located just south of the Gay Village. A few private rooms with en suite are available. ✆ *76 Church St • Map L4 • 416 971 4440 • www.hostelling toronto. com • $–$$*

Hostelling International Niagara Falls

A short walk from the falls, this hostel is especially well kept. No private baths, but some private rooms, along with dorms and four-bed rooms. ✆ *4549 Cataract Ave, Niagara Falls • Map Q3 • 905 357 0770 • www. hostellingniagara • $*

General Index

Acknowledgments

The Authors
Lorraine Johnson is the author of several books and coauthor of Dorling Kindersley's Eyewitness guide to Chicago. She also writes regularly for magazines on gardening and environmental issues. She lives in Toronto.

Barbara Hopkinson is a writer and editor who has directed a wide range of international publishing projects. She lives in Toronto.

Produced by International Book Productions Inc., Toronto

Editorial Director
Barbara Hopkinson
Art Editor James David Ellis
Senior Editor Judy Phillips
Senior DTP Designer
Dietmar Kokemohr
Photo Research and Permissions
Sheila Hall
Proofreader Ken Ramstead
Indexer Barbara Sale Schon
Photographer Cylla von Tiedemann
Additional Photographers Rough Guides/Enrique Uranga

SPECIAL THANKS: Raj Rama, Ontario Tourism Marketing Partnership; Lou Seiler, Casa Loma; Michael Snow; Renée Tratch, Royal Ontario Museum

AT DORLING KINDERSLEY
Senior Art Editor
Marisa Renzullo
Senior Editor Kathryn Lane
Publishing Manager Kate Poole
Publisher Douglas Amrine
Senior Cartographic Editor
Casper Morris
Senior DTP Designer Jason Little
Production Rita Sinha
Maps Simonetta Giori, Dominic Beddow (Draughtsman Ltd)
Picture Researchers
Rhiannon Furbear, Ellen Root, Romaine Werblow

Revisions Team Louise Abbott, Namrata Adhwaryu, Mark Bailey, Lydia Baillie, Marta Bescos Sanchez, Sonal Bhatt, Ilona Biro, Caroline Elliker, Mariana Evmolpidou, Sumita Khatwani, Kathryn Lane, Maite Lantaron, Nicola Malone, Hayley Maher, Alison McGill, Jane Mundy, Catherine Palmi, Marianne Petrou, Louis Pin, Mani Ramaswamy, Quadrum Solutions, Susana Smith